THE AMERICAN PEOPLE'S MONEY

A volume in the Hyperion reprint series
THE RADICAL TRADITION IN AMERICA

THE
AMERICAN PEOPLE'S MONEY

BY

HON. IGNATIUS DONNELLY.

Author of "Cæsar's Column," "The Great Cryptogram," "Dr. Huguet," Etc

---

"You may fool part of the people all the time, or all the people part
of the time, but you cannot fool all the people all the time."
—*Abraham Lincoln.*

HYPERION PRESS, INC.
Westport, Connecticut

Published in 1896 by Laird & Lee, Publishers, Chicago
Hyperion reprint edition 1976
Library of Congress Catalog Number 75-311
ISBN 0-88355-215-9
Printed in the United States of America

Library of Congress Cataloging in Publication Data

Donnelly, Ignatius, 1831-1901.
  The American people's money.

  (The Radical tradition in America)
  Reprint of the 1895 ed. published by Laird & Lee,
Chicago, which was issued as no. 141 of The Pastime
series.
  1. Silver question. 2. Money — United States —
History. I. Title. II. Series: The Pastime series ;
no. 141.
HG556.D68   1975   332.4'973   75-311
ISBN 0-88355-215-9

THE AMERICAN PEOPLE'S MONEY

CHAPTER I

SCENE:—A palace sleeping car on an overland train from Chicago to the Pacific. Great bustle and confusion; crowds rushing through and treading on each others' feet. People kissing and bidding good-bye in the aisles—to the obstruction of all the rest—when they might just as well have done their farewelling in the depot. Husbands and wives parting with tears,—with internal consolatory reflections. Bags, valises, bundles, umbrellas gradually crawling into corners and adjusting themselves to them. Colored porters moving around, sombre and mysterious as Othello, when he was about to do the business for Desdemona. Grave looking brakesmen and conductors, with cabalistic gold letters on their caps, and semi-military uniform—the children think they own the railroad, and they feel like it themselves.

The ringing of the bells and tooting of the engine, with a great deal of unnecessary uproar, and the huge grandson of the old stage coach moves slowly out of the depot. The passengers draw a sigh of relief and settle back in their seats—some put on their skull-caps and slippers. Each man and woman looks about at his or her neighbors—the men at the faces, the women at the clothes.

In section No. 7 two men faced each other. Both were of about middle life; both were well-dressed; both looked well-to-do; and yet they represented two widely different

9

types of the genus *Homo*. The one facing the engine
(which showed he had the right to the lower berth), was
evidently a business man; gloves on hands; a high silk
hat; broadcloth garments; a clear-cut, keen face, with
penetrating eyes and firm mouth.

He was studying the person on the opposite seat, (the
tenant of the upper berth), and these were his reflections:

"Respectable looking man—not poor—lives in the
country—has the bronzed skin and large chest which
comes from having acres of space to supply him with the
finer elements of the atmosphere. Large frame—six feet
high. That slouch hat never was made in Chicago. Good
nose, and large, broad brow too. No fool. Glad he has
the upper berth. Fewer thieves among the middle-aged
than among the young. Why is that? Don't like to
have one of our modern scamps too near me. The criminal class now is largely composed of those half way
between boy and man. Some of them would cut a traveler's throat for five dollars. Wonder if he is going
through. I must get acquainted with him. It will be
safe to do so."

"The car is crowded, sir."

"Yes," replied the other, "I suppose a great many are
going through to the coast."

"Probably so. Do you go through?"

"Yes."

"Do you live there?"

"No; I am from central Illinois. But I have a son
who owns a fruit farm, near Sacramento, and I am going
out to visit him."

"As we will be together for several days we might as
well become acquainted," and he handed the other his
card.

It read: "James Hutchinson, president of the Traders' and Mechanics' Bank, Chicago."

"I have no card," replied the other, "but my name is Hugh Sanders, farmer, of Shelbyville, Shelby county, Illinois."

"Do you find farming profitable?" inquired Mr. Hutchinson.

"No; I can't say I do," was the reply. "Nothing is profitable now-a-days but your business of money-lending. Fortunately for me I made my money during the war, and soon after it, when prices were high; and of late years I have rented my lands for a share of the crop, and thus have taken no chances, and have kept out of debt. If I had farmed it myself I should probably be in the same boat with the rest of them. As it is I have a good lot of land and some money out at interest. Present conditions are such that the man who does nothing is better off than the man who ventures and works hard and produces something. Society rewards the idler and punishes the toiler."

"I fear you are a pessimist," said the banker.

"You mean a 'crank,'" replied the farmer, "but you are too polite to speak it right out. I suppose I am. Years of observation have led me to the conclusion that the world is in bad shape, and likely to grow worse."

"Why," said the other, "there has never been a time in the history of the world when wealth increased more rapidly, or the productive power of industry was greater."

"Yes, I admit that; but it only intensifies the wrong conditions. If the reverse were true—if all wealth was shrinking—no man could complain because he suffered his just share of the universal calamity. And if labor, from some cause, produced only one-tenth as much as it did thirty or fifty years ago, the laborer would be ashamed to protest. But when those who produce the wealth do not get all, or even a reasonable part, of what they create; but, on the contrary, find what they have is slipping away from them, then it is no wonder they complain. The only wonder is that they are as patient as they are. The intelligent laborer says to himself: 'This machine I am using enables me to do ten times as much work as formerly, but I do not get ten times as much pay; I do not get even as much as I did then. And there are a hundred unemployed men hanging around the factory doors, or looking in at the windows, with eager, hungry faces, ready to take my place if I object, and work for less than I require to support myself and family.'"

"But that is the great law of supply and demand," said Mr. Hutchinson. "You might just as well try to amend the attraction of gravitation by an act of the legislature, as to interfere with a great economic law. Competition must necessarily force down wages, according to the 'iron law of wages,' to the lowest point of compensation for which the laborer will be able to live, perform his work and raise another to take his place when his time has come. This rule runs through all nature. Darwin calls it the 'survival of the fittest.' The man who can work for fifty cents a day survives the man who works for a dollar a day; and the man who will work for twenty-five cents a day will take the place of the man who will not work for less than fifty cents."

"Precisely," said the other, "and the man who will work for ten cents must eventually supplant the man who asks for a quarter."

"Exactly."

"And there is no limit to it?"

" None whatever. The operation of the law is inflexible and inexorable."

" Then it follows that as the great mass of mankind are toilers with muscles, the great mass of mankind must be reduced to the lowest possible condition compatible with continued existence?'

" Of course."

" So that the Chinaman who works for six cents a day and lives on a diet of rice, flavored with an occasional rat, is a type of what the American citizen of the producing class is to be in the near future?"

" It seems so; the law is inflexible."

" But does not Darwin admit that the human race, by reason of its intelligence, rises above the limitations of his great theory? He shows that the too great increase of the lower animals has, for countless ages, been kept in check by the wild beasts that preyed upon them, and by the contagious diseases which infected them. But man, with his big, active, bold, cunning brain, proceeded to exterminate, by pitfalls, arrows, spears, snares, poisons, the wild beasts, until he has driven them off three-fourths of the earth's surface. He turned the tables on them; and instead of their living off him and his offspring, he dragged their carcasses and those of their young into his den or cave, and dined upon them.

"And of late years his masterful intellect and keen penetration has led him to discover the minute forms of life, which, swarming in his system, produce what we call diseases; and he is able now to check their ravages; even to set one kind of microscopic creature to pursue and devour another; so that plagues which formerly swept whole continents nearly bare of human inhabitants are now comparatively harmless.

"Thus, you perceive, that the doctrine of 'the survival of the fittest' does not stand when it comes in conflict with human intelligence. Go look at the huge bones of the monstrous lions, tigers, wolves and bears found in the caves of Europe. Where are their progeny to-day? There is none. They are exterminated. Then look around for the posterity of the naked savages, armed with clubs and flint weapons, who exterminated them, and you behold the swarming, cultured, highly-civilized inhabitants of London, Paris and Berlin. Primitive man had not the size of his giant foes, nor their strength, nor their swiftness, but he had intellect, and to intellect all laws yield.

"Man not only exterminated the wild animals, but he has put bits in the mouths of the cruel aristocracy which once made him a slave; and he crossed the wide Atlantic to found a government on this continent from which all that cruel breed of beasts might be excluded.

"And, if necessary, the free man will exterminate any new aristocracy which may rise up to reduce him to universal poverty, (to six cents a day and rice and rats), just as he blotted out the fierce creatures of prehistoric times. Your philosophers may speculate about your great economic laws, under which the majority are to be enslaved by the minority; but the highest law on this earth is the law of the human intelligence, which bends all things to itself, and which claims for each a fair share of the joys and blessing of life.

> ' This will footpath all your seas;
> Will track your lightning to its lair of cloud,
> Lay flat your forests; master, with a frown,
> Your lion in his fasting; and fetch down
> Your eagle flying.'"

The speaker's eyes flashed as he spoke, and Mr. Hutchinson looked at him with astonishment. He was a revelation to him. He thought what would not ten million men accomplish who felt as this man did—even if they could not express themselves as clearly.

"But, my dear sir," he said, "is your view of life the correct one? Does not the patience with which the lower classes sink into servitude, all over the world, and humbly submit to their lot, show that they are not entitled to anything better? Must there not be a cultured, intelligent class, for whom the good things of this world are intended? These are the men who encourage and reward art; who read the books of the great authors; who cultivate science; purchase the works of the immortal painters; build opera houses and listen to the distinguished musicians; these are the representatives of the highest civilization."

"Very true," replied the other, "but we differ as to how extensive that class should be. You would confine it to the money-dealers and their families—a few thousand in number. We believe that, under a proper system of government, the great bulk of mankind can be brought up to that level. We recognize the fact that the mental qualities which give a man success, in this scramble for spoil, are the very things which unfit him and his breed to play the part of public exemplars of a generous age. You cannot make a race of artists, statesmen or philanthropists of a people who have achieved success simply because there was in their blood an inherited monkey-like instinct to grab everything their paws could reach.

"And, when you come to consider it, how shallow appear the vanities of the greatly rich. A man cannot eat more than a reasonable quantity of plain food, except

at the cost of his health and the shortening of his life. He cannot drink anything but pure and simple beverages without disordering his system, producing sickness, and hurrying himself into the grave. We read that one of the Rothschilds, possessed of immense wealth, was taken sick, not long since, and sent for the best doctor he could find. The doctor told him the impairment of his health was due to his riches and high living, and that if he would live, he must cast aside his possessions, so far as his personal enjoyment was concerned, and come down to the condition of the beggar that begs from door to door. Rothschild concluded that life without luxury was preferable to a death bed with millions; and so he is seen, barefooted and bareheaded, tramping the roads of his estate and living on bread and milk. That is all he can get out of life, despite his vast wealth. That is all Christ and Socrates had—but how different the results of their life-work. They blessed, and benefited mankind by their example and teachings, while every Rothschild that has ever lived has simply degraded humanity and lessened its happiness.

"And what is it to gather around one a great variety of decorations and adornments—to rest their superiority upon the gimcrackery they can collect. Is the interior spirit greatened by piling on its temporary shell a heap of things for which it has no use whatever? A man cannot wear more than one suit of clothes at a time if he has a thousand. The distinguised family of Ten Broeck, so we are told, takes its name from the fact that the original ancestor was the proud possessor of ten pairs of breeches, which he wore all at the same time! Here is your true aristocrat. Observe the breechless fellows—the savages —looking on him with envy or reverence.

" Human happiness, in this degenerate age, seems to
consist in having what somebody else wants; and the
more urgently they want it the keener is the satisfaction
of the fellow who withholds it. Ten Broeck may be
inconvenienced by trying to locomote encased in those ten
pairs of breeches, but how delighted he is t. think that
the ten savages have not even a breechcloth to cover their
nakedness. That compensates him for the chafing of his
legs. He would fight to the death rather than divide with
the breechesless ones. And his posterity was so proud
of the fact that he had ten pairs of breeches, and wore
them all at once, that they represented the distinction in
the family name; and there it will stand as long as one of
the breed survives. There you have a type of the true
monopolist—to hold on to something, for vanity sake or
selfishness, which is of no use to him and a veritable injury
to retain. If Jay Gould had been content with $100,000
instead of $100,000,000, he would probably have lived
twenty years longer. He rotted prematurely to obtain
that which enslaved and destroyed him, and which he
had to leave behind. If the soul retains consciousness
and the passions of this life, how wretched must be the
feelings of the spirit of one who has lived purely to plunder his fellow men, to realize that he has no pockets under
his wings, and that his ghostly fingers can grab and
carry away nothing? Although his impalpable substance
may pass into the treasure vaults of the world; the gold,
the silver, the jewels are safe from his greed. He will
look upon the poor man at work in the fields and weep
to think that no longer can he compel him to work for
his profit. He will see the trooping millions of men and
women going to their daily work, and tear his hair with

The Ghost of the Dead Plutocrat

rage, to think that while they are plundered of all but a
bare subsistence he can get none of the spoil.

" And then, if the ghost takes any interest in posterity,
how it must agonize him to see the possessions, which he
sacrificed everything to collect, squandered by the vice
and shallowness of his posterity; or to observe that the
same greed, which in him, directed by shrewdness and
cunning, gave him fortune, misdirected in his children or

Dives' Posterity

his children's children is leading them to crime and the
prison and the scaffold; for an evil nature is more certain
to descend from generation to generation than the millions
which he left them.

" The gospel of grab, incited by vanity, will eventuate
in ridiculous vanity when the necessity to grab is gone;
and the posterity of the successful adventurer will signal-
ize themselves with antics of pretension that would disgrace a couple of gorillas.

"The best testimony to the shallowness of the qualities which make men rich is the character of their offspring. Look at the English nobility which, in these latter days, is principally of plutocratic origin:

> ' "Brewers and bakers, men of hideous omen,
> Auriferous fellows of immense abdomen,
> Flashy directors with their diamond rings—
> Such is the sum of our six hundred kings.'

"And see the breed of cattle they are producing—the Oscar Wildes and the Queensberry stock—guilty of practices which a brute beast would be incapable of. Are we to exchange the glorious dreams of the poets and philanthropists, of a universal lifting up of the whole human family, for a few thousand bestial aud degraded creatures like these? Shall we turn back the wheels of time and destroy our splendid civilization, and concentrate the sun's energies and God's largesses in raising up a lot of Sodomites?

"The noblest sight that is unrolled beneath the eyes of the Creator is a mighty concourse of people, none vastly rich, none greatly poor, but all intelligent, educated, industrious; gaining abundance by honest toil; with none to despoil them, none to molest or make them afraid; but each and all loving man and praising God. This is a picture over which the angels hang with delight, and which lights up the face of Divinity with smiles. This is a grander sight than all the hundreds of millions of suns of the universe.

"But how dreadful is the picture when that vast concourse of the world's inhabitants are like martyrs in a pit, with the lions and tigers of greed and cunning and cruelty leaping upon and devouring them, while the ground is

wet with their blood, and the heavens ring with their
pitiful lamentations. And that is the condition of the
great mass of mankind to-day. In their horrible distress
they faint and die; nay, they kill each other; they even
cut and stab and mangle themselves to escape out of this
sentient world, which God had intended shall be so
gracious and beautiful.

"And how dreadful is it to think that a race of beings
so capable, so masterful,

"'The beauty of the world, the paragon of animals,'

"who have conquered wind and waves and heat and cold,
and made them their instruments; who have dug out of
the bosom of patient nature her hidden and secret powers
and make them lightning-like servants; who have chained
steam and electricity, and sent them, like the genii of
Arabian fable, over all the globe, annihilating time and
space. How dreadful, I say, is it that this superb race
of demi-gods should fall down into the abyss like a
trapped lion, and lie there wounded and howling?"

"Your picture, my friend," said the banker, "is
strongly drawn, but it is an exaggeration. Mankind is
not in such a lost condition as you represent. But suppose it is, are not the results unavoidable? Is it not the
work of Providence? Are the rich responsible for the
evil state of the world?"

"It angers me," said the other, "to hear the sins and
blunders of men laid on the shoulders of Omnipotence.

"'The fault, dear Brutus, is not in our stars,
But in ourselves, that we are underlings.'

"I believe it is in the power of man to make this earth
a paradise or a hell. I believe the resources of this planet

are adequate to support in the highest degree of comfort fifty times the population that now inhabits it.   It is God's intention that we should reach that elevated condition; but he has given us intelligence and he expects us to work out the problem for ourselves.   He will not save us by old-fashioned miracles.   When he intervenes it is through the minds of men—in great tidal waves of universal feelings,—and in our vanity we think we did it all ourselves. 'It is the glory of God to conceal a thing and the glory of man to find it out?'

"But I see the porter is looking over his nose at us, and thinks we ought to go to bed."

" Well, let us retire," said Mr. Hutchinson, " and we will renew the conversation in the morning.   I am interested in your views, although I am sure you are altogether wrong.   Good night."

" Good night."

CHAPTER II.

THE SECOND DAY.

" Good morning, Mr. Hutchinson," said the farmer, "I hope you had a good night's rest and enjoyed your breakfast."

" Yes ; the air seems to improve as we go west."

" We are rising gradually onto the table-land of the continent.   We are getting into the great breathing spaces.   Henry Ward Beecher, the first time he inhaled this kind of air, drew a long breath and said,—'Ah ! this is beefsteak !' He was right.   The animal organism is fed as much by the air as it is by the earth; but some

atmospheres are more nourishing than others, even as
some earths are.   Lord Bacon wrote, at one time,—' I live
upon the swordpoint of a sharp air.'   And how beauti-
full is Banquo's picture:

> ' This guest of summer,
> The temple-haunting martlet, does approve,
> By his loved mansionry that the heaven's breath
> Smells wooingly here ; no julty, frieze,
> Buttress nor coign of vantage, but this bird
> Hath made his pendant bed and procreant cradle:
> Where they most breed and haunt, I have observed
> The air is delicate.'

"This intercontinental table-land of America, lying higher
up, near the clouds, surcharged with electricity and fed
by the most exquisite parts of the atmosphere, will produce the grandest race of men and women that has ever
inhabited the planet.   They will be the masters of the
continent, if not of the world.   Observe the height, vigor,
activity and breadth between the ears and eyes of the new
generation that is springing up,—they are extraordinary."

"Then you don't think the Plutocracy is going to
enslave them?   You were very pessimistic last night,"
said Mr. Hutchinson, sarcastically.

"No; they will do their best.   But the human family
having once risen out of serfdom cannot be forced back
into it.   There will be struggles and conflicts, perhaps
revolutions and wars ; sometimes the people will be prostrate upon their backs, chained hand and foot ; and again
they will be up with flashing and unobscured eyes, striking right and left, like a thresher with his flail.   The con-
test may terminate in a few years, or it may run through
centuries ; but ' there is a power in nature which makes
for goodness, and evil is not to be our god.   The Ever-

lasting Justice will not permit the millions to starve that the thousands may be overwhelmed with hog-like super-fluity.''

''Let us avoid generalizations,'' said the banker, ''and come down to practical details. You said last night that the evils which men endure are due to misgovernment. What proof have you of the truth of that statement?''

''Compare Ireland and New Hampshire. The former is one of the richest bodies of land on earth ; fed by the showers of the gulf stream ; indeed an emerald land forever green ; where the temperature rarely goes below the freezing point or rises to tropical heat ; a land known to the ancients as a region where two crops could be raised in the same year. And yet what is it? A land of

beggars, where the population has fallen off one-half in
fifty years, while everywhere else on earth it is increasing.
Why? Because of misgovernment. The country has
been in the hands of plunderers, and has been governed
in their interest, not in the interest of the producing
classes of the island. The people are merely instruments
to turn the fatness of the land into money for the idlers.
Parnell said you could travel for twenty miles, in parts of
Ireland, without seeing a human being. Redpath said
that there were no dogs in large sections of that unhappy
land because the wretched people could not spare the food
to sustain a dog!

"Then, turn and look at New Hampshire! Masses of
barren mountains where a hungry eagle would starve to
death; the soil producing an annual crop of stones sufficient to fence it into five-acre lots, with enough to spare
on every thousand acres to build a city. The farmers it
is said sharpen the noses of their sheep to enable them to
reach in between the stones for the scattered blades of
grass. And yet New Hampshire is a land of prosperity,
a land of culture, a land of wealth, a land of millionaires.
I came from there. You will hear the piano playing in
mansions beside rocky roads where there is scarcely room
to turn a wagon; while the railway cars are packed with
an endless concourse of bright, handsome, intelligent
people, perpetually moving to and fro in search of business or pleasure.

"Why the difference? It is simply because New
Hampshire has not been governed by non-residents or
idlers, but by her own people. They have taken advantage of every opportunity; they have developed every
resource; and they have reached out and gathered in the
spoil of distant and more favored regions."

"But is not religion responsible for this difference between Ireland and New Hampshire? The Irish are mostly Catholics."

"I know," said Mr. Sanders, "that that argument is often used; but if you will stop and think for a moment the Belgians are as Catholic as the Irish, and they are the most industrious and prosperous race of toilers in Europe. Next to them come the French peasants, dwelling on their one acre and five acre farms, given them by the great revolution, and cultivating them to the highest pitch of perfection. They are all Catholics; and in the midst of even these disastrous times France is flourishing. Catholic Austria is no whit inferior to Protestant Prussia in industry or economy. Indeed, how is it possible that a man's belief as to the presence or non-presence of God in the sacrificial wafer can affect the quantity of meal in his flour-barrel or the thickness of the coat on his back?"

"But their race may account for it," said Mr. Hutchinson, "the Irish are Celts."

"So are the Welsh and the French and the Belgians and the Highland Scotch. The Irish of to-day are the most composite race in the world. Before the discovery of America Ireland was the most western land of Europe, where all the converging lines of migration met, as they are meeting to-day in these United States. Phœnicia, Greece, Italy, Spain contributed to the original stock. One sixth of the Irish words are Basque. All the coast towns of Ireland: Dublin, Cork, Drogheda, Waterford, etc., were settled by the Danes, Swedes and Norwegians. Dublin was a Norwegian city for four hundred years and nothing spoken in it but the tongue of the Northmen. The Scandinavians held possession of the island for generations; and a Gothic soldier was in every Irish house. No, sir; the cry of race is the excuse for injustice. It is amusing to hear a little, swarthy, black-eyed Englishman, with all the insignia of Celtic-Briton blood, trying to prove that a raw-boned, six-foot, red-headed, fair-skinned, blue-eyed Irishman, with Goth written all over him, is unfit for anything but poverty and oppression—because he is a Celt!

"No, sir," continued Mr. Sanders, "the difference between Ireland and New Hampshire represents the difference between good government and bad government. The statute-book is at the bottom of everything. Ireland is naturally rich--and a land of paupers. New Hampshire, like Eden after the Fall, is a place of stones and thistles, but she is the home of gentlemen and princes. The time was when we Americans, filled with our inherited English prejudices, mocked the poor Irishman, working on railroads and in ditches, and living on potatoes. But the English greed which brought Paddy to this condition, has now reduced millions of our own high-spirited race to even lower conditions. They cannot get work on railroads, or ditches, or anything else, but are living on the thin soup of public charity; while our cities are preparing, under the Pingree plan, to bring the free men of this country to the same sustenance of potatoes, as a steady diet, for which we used to despise poor landlord-impoverished Paddy. The Irishman, trained for generations in the school of English oppression and starvation, his stomach ensmalled by poverty, is better able to stand the persimmon diet of the present day than the child of the Declaration of Independence, who comes to it for the first time."

"Persimmon diet!" said Mr. Hutchinson, "what do you mean by that?"

"Have you not heard the old story?" replied Mr. Sanders. "A regiment of confederate soldiers, during the civil war, were marching through a region of country that had been swept bare by the contending armies. They were half starved. The colonel rode up to a persimmon tree, and found one of his command up in the tree, eating the unripe fruit.

"'Bill,' said he 'what are you doing there? Those persimmons are not fit to eat.'

"'I know it, colonel,' responded Bill, 'but I am trying to pucker up my stomach to the size of my rations.'"

"Very good," said Mr. Hutchinson, "but really, my friend, what has the volume of currency got to do with the prosperity of the people?

John Bull.—"What are you doing up in that tree, Uncle Samuel?"
Uncle Samuel.—"I am making ready—I am trying to adjust my bi-metallic stomach to your darned mono-metallic rations."

If a man can buy as much with fifty cents as he could with a dollar, what difference does it make to him?"

"In other words," replied the farmer, "if the confederate soldier could have sufficiently contracted his stomach by the aid of the persimmons, he could have lived as well on a half ration as as a whole one, and been equally vigorous and hearty. Is that what you mean?"

"No; that is an illustration, not an argument."

"An illustration," replied the other, "is oftentimes the highest argument. The parables of Christ made millions of converts whom his logic would never have reached. Our clearest thoughts are those that take the form of living figures. God thinks in facts and man in pictures. Weakness diffuses itself into theories; strength boils the theories down into an incident.

"Now," he continued, "let us test your proposition. You intimate it can do no harm to reduce the volume of the world's currency one-half—that mankind will adjust itself to it. If this be so, then the same argument will hold true if we cut it down to one-fourth. Why not? Where does the contraction cease to be reasonable and become unreasonable? And if you can cut it down to one-fourth, why not to one-tenth? Is there any limit to the adjustability of humanity to its environment? If so, what is it? Now, if this be true, why not abolish all forms of money, and fall back on primeval barter? Man once existed without currency. Why can he not do so again?"

"That would never do," replied Mr. Hutchinson. "That would end all borrowing and lending, all bonds and mortgages, all drafts, bills of exchange and promissory notes. It is absurd to talk of going back to barter. The banks would all have to close. They could not take

wheat and potatoes on deposit. The lady who went shop-
ping would have to fill her carriage with chickens,
turkeys, quarters of beef, legs of mutton, turnips and
cabbages.   If a man took a street car, he would have to
have a bag on his back, and when the conductor came
around he would haul out two or three ears of corn to
pay his fare. When the workman received his week's
wages in meat and vegetables and cloth, he would have
to spend another week to trade them off.   All the great
staple crops, instead of being shipped, as now, in bulk,
to the central markets to be sold for money, would be
broken up into fragments and fly backwards and forward
in carts and cars like a weaver's shuttle, to answer the
infinite necessities of many millions of people. Why,

such a system
would end civiliza-
tion and send us all
back to barbarism.
Every citizen would
have to have a cart
for a pocket book.
No, no; that would
never do. The pro-
position is absurd."
   "I am glad that
you perceive that,"
responded Mr.
Sanders, "for the
point I desire to
make is, *that every
reduction of the*

"Primeval barter, what we are coming to."

*money of a country below an adequate per capita for the
needs of the people, is an approximation toward the con-*

dition of no money at all. It is worse ; for humanity, if there was no currency in existence, nor pretence of any, would speedily adjust itself to its environment ; and would have no more need for money than the savage of Dahomey has. But when you possess a state of development requiring an adequate supply of currency, and, at the same time, there are limitations placed upon it dragging down the people toward savagery, the human race is caught be-

"*The results of an insufficient currency.*"

tween the upper and nether millstones of civilization and barbarism, and ground into agony and wretchedness."

"But what would you call an adequate supply of currency?" inquired the banker.

"That is a difficult question to answer," replied the farmer. "It must depend upon the condition of the people. If they are unprogressive, lethargic, and peasant-like it would require much less currency than that needed for a highly intellectual and intensely active people, turning out, with the aid of great inventions, an immense quantity of productions of all kinds. In December, 1865, Secretary of the Treasury McCulloch reported to Congress that ' the people are now comparatively free from debt.' The workman owned his home and the farmer his farm, unencumbered by mortgages. There was work for every one. There were no tramps in the land."

"What caused that condition?" asked the banker.

"Simply the fact that we had over sixty dollars per capita, of money, in circulation."

"That is impossible," replied Mr. Hutchinson. "We had not half that amount. We have nearly as much money in circulation now as we had then."

"What makes you think so?"

"Why, that is the universal testimony of our daily press."

THE PER CAPITA OF CURRENCY IN 1865.

"A consensus of opinion," replied Mr. Sanders, "on the part of the daily press of the United States, clearly establishes the opposite proposition; and the more earnest and emphatic they are the greater the misrepresentation. There are not more than half a dozen papers that are an exception to this rule."

"That," said the banker, "is the view espoused by the anarchists. They call it the hireling press."

"I have nothing to do with the anarchists," said the other, "but a man may clearly perceive the cause of an evil and yet advocate an unwise remedy. I rest my assertion upon the following facts.

"The men of moderate means do not have vast sums to invest in such precarious undertakings as daily newspapers. You remember, doubtless, the story of the man who sold his soul to the devil, on condition that he should have all the money he wanted. If Satan failed to meet his expenditures, however extravagant, the contract was to be at an end. After some years of riotous and prodigal profusion, the devil paying the bills promptly, our adventurer, seeing the end drawing near, determined to try to 'bust' Beelzebub. He began by gambling and

losing wholesale. The devil never winced. Then he
took to speculating in western real estate, still the money
was advanced promptly. Then he built and operated a
theatre; the devil grumbled but paid up. Then he
established a daily paper. At the end of six months his
Satanic majesty told him he could go to—heaven ! That
his darned old soul wasn't worth what it was costing him,

> " 'And Lucifer fled to his home again,
> On the wings of a blasting hurricane ;
> And left old Armonel to die
> And sleep in the odor of sanctity.'

" The Devil broke."

"A man by honest industry can make a comfortable living and a moderate competency for old age; that is all.
If he desires a million he must make tens of thousands or

hundreds of thousands of other men work for him, and take all the fruits of their toil *above a mere living*. Hence when it comes to establishing a daily newspaper, at a cost of a hundred thousand, or five hundred thousand dollars, the founders must be rich men. And if they go into such an enterprise it is to increase their wealth. And to do this the conditions which gave them their opportunities must be maintained; and hence the paper must oppose all reform measures that would protect the many from the exactions of the few. And the friends of one kind of oppression are compelled, necessarily, to unite with those of all other forms of oppression ; and hence we have a gigantic power, undreamed of by our ancestors, which holds possession of all access to the brains and beliefs of the multitude, and is misleading them to their ruin. It is a diabolical contrivance and one of the greatest of the dangers which now threaten civilization. To get at the truth the people have to 'read between the lines,' or depend on books, pamphlets and the weekly newspapers; and even a great part of these latter are but a weak echo of the dailies, — the editors bought to betray the people with some such trivial bribe as a free railroad ticket. Hence the outburst of pamphlets, which characterized the era of Queen Ann, is being repeated in this our present age. It is the effort of the chained and imprisoned intellect of man to obtain a hearing, despite the plutocratic power which has taken possession of all the avenues of public enlightenment."

"This is all very pretty," said Mr. Hutchinson, " but it does not answer my assertion, that the people of the United States have as large a circulating medium to-day as they had in 1865."

"Well, I shall try to answer it," replied Mr. Sanders. "Let us take up first the question as to how much circulation we had in 1865.

"The Treasurer of the United States," here he consulted a little book which he drew from his pocket, "Mr. F. E. Spinner, he of the complicated signature, on page 244 of the finance report, 1869, says:

OUTSTANDING CIRCULATION.

"Recapitulation of all kinds of government papers that were issued as money, or that were, in any way, used as a circulating medium:

"Seven and three-tenths notes; temporary loan certificates; certificates of indebtedness; six per cent. compound interest notes; gold certificates; three per cent. certificates; old two year six per cent. notes; one year five per cent notes; two year five per cent. notes; two year five per cent. coupon notes; demand notes; legal tender notes, and fractional currency."

"On pages 27 and 28 Messages and Documents, 1867–8, a public-debt statement shows that the following amounts of indebtedness, which the Treasurer of the United States declared were used as money, were in existence:

Certificates of indebtedness	$ 85,093,000.00
Five per cent. legal tender notes . . .	33,954,230.00
Compound interest legal tender notes . .	217,024,160.00
Seven-thirty notes	830,000,000.00
United States notes	433,160,569.00
Fractional currency	26,344,742.51
Total	$1,625,576,701.51

"These were the obligations of the government, issued by the government, and used as money. Of the whole amount $634,138,-959.00 were made by law legal tender. But in addition to these we must count in the gold and silver, the state bank notes, the

"How the American people get their ideas."

national bank notes and the demand notes which were in circulation. These were:

Gold, at a premium, used to pay duties on imports	$189,000,000.00
Silver (estimated)	9,500,000.00
State bank notes	142,919,638.00
National bank notes	146,137,860.00
Demand notes	472,603.00
Total	$488,030,101.00

"If we add this to the foregoing we have a grand total of $2,113,606,802.51. The population of the United States, in 1865, was 34,748,000. Divide this total into the money total of $2,113,606,802.51 and it gives $67.26 for each inhabitant. That was our *per capita* then."

"But," said Mr. Hutchinson, "you have counted in $830,000,000 of 'seven-thirty notes' as money. They were not."

"What were they?" asked the farmer.

"They were bonds."

"Why then were they called 'seven-thirty *notes*' instead of 'seven-thirty *bonds*'?" replied Mr. Sanders. "They were not printed in the form of bonds, but of *notes*. And the interest was made $7.30 cents a year on $100; or twice 365; which is equal to two cents per day; so that when the notes passed from hand it was easy for the parties to count up the accrued interest and allow in their dealings for it. This was the reason that rate of $7.30 was agreed upon. And that these 7.30 notes did pass from hand to hand there is no question. A number of persons have testified, in the newspapers, during this discussion, to receiving them as money and paying then out as money. The Secretary of the Treasury, W. P.

Fessenden, on page 206 of his report, made the following statement:

"'More fully to accomplish his purpose, the Secretary resolved to avail himself of a wish expressed by many army officers and soldiers, through the paymasters, and offered to such as desired to receive their pay seven-thirty notes of small denominations. He was gratified to find that these notes were readily taken to a large amount. The whole amount thus disposed of exceeded $20,000,000; and the Secretary has great satisfaction in stating his belief that the disposal thus made was not only a relief to the treasury, but a benefit to the recipients as affording them an easy mode of transmitting funds to their families.'

"This emphatically settles the question as to whether or not they were used as money. They paid off our armies in the midst of the great struggle for the unity of our territory. But their use was not confined to our officers and soldiers; they were taken by the creditors of the government and readily passed from hand to hand, carrying their accumulating interest with them. It simply shows how desperate are the straits of the monometallists, and how unscrupulous are their methods when they would attempt to deny a fact that is within the knowledge and memory of hundreds of thousands of those yet living. A cause must be bad indeed that has to be defended by such flagrant falsehoods."

"But," said the banker, "the supply of currency was too great in 1865. It had to be reduced."

CONTRACTION OF THE CURRENCY.

"Not necessarily," said the other. "No one complained of too much money. The merchants and business men were more prosperous than they had ever been before in any age or country. The very capitalists were flourishing, for there were enterprises inviting investment on every hand, and every investment was prosperous. There were in 1865 but 530 failures in the United States; in 1878, five years after the demonetization of silver, the number of failures had increased to 12,000!"

" But, surely," said Mr. Hutchinson, " the contraction of the currency was not the cause of this tremendous change? It was due to the reaction from an era of over-speculation; it was the sickness that follows the debauch."

" That is the usual comparison," replied the other. " You gentlemen seem to think that prosperity and happiness are a species of drunkenness, and that man's normal condition is wretchedness and misery. And you so argue because in all the past ages the afflicted human family, darkened by ignorance, terrified by superstition, robbed by power, the prey of kings and queens, dukes and barons, tricksters and usurers, overrun by armies or engaged in almost perpetual war, merely survived on the planet, and thought it was happiness to be permitted to barely live. Hence they are ready to believe that an outburst of prosperity, such as followed our civil war, due to that $67 per capita, was a drunken debauch, a lunatical dream, and that the sooner it was ended, and they got back to their ancestral wretchedness, the better for them. But why should a period of universal prosperity and advancement be unnatural or unreasonable, when the highest, most energetic, industrious and civilized people of the earth were spreading over the larger part of a continent, creating states, counties, cities, highways, and, armed with the marvelous powers of steam and electricity, releasing the stored-up, million-year-old resources of the fields and forests and mines? To stop such a people in mid-career is the greatest crime ever committed on the globe. And it is adding the gravest insult to the profoundest villainy for a lot of money-lenders to tell the inhabitants of the conquered nation that their natural and proper condition is a state of helpless poverty and suffering. It is an army of Gullivers, giants, tied down by a score or two of little, cunning Lilliputians, in the midst of their wrecked resources; not only overthrown, but lied to and deceived, which is the saddest and most disgraceful part of it."

"Very well said, from your standpoint," interjected Mr. Hutchinson, "but I do not see that you prove that a decrease of the currency produces the ruin of the people. Even in these hard times the banks are overflowing with money. There is more currency than the people can use."

"Very true," said the other, "but there is more blood in the head of the man stricken with apoplexy than he can make any use of. He dies from the unnatural engorgement. This country is in a state of apoplexy. The money has all gone to the banks. The extremities of the nation are cold and pulseless. The doctor who would say that the apoplectic patient was in an extraordinarily healthy condition because he had more blood in his head than any other man in three counties would be called a fool, and a fit subject for the insane asylum. Money is the life-blood of trade and social intercourse. It should flow with equal force to all parts of the body politic. Then the eyes are bright, the cheeks are red, the digestion is good, the footsteps quick and springy, and the whole man fulfilling the functions God gave him to perform. But when the money is all in the banks the country lies upon its back, powerless, helpless, while its stertorous breathing shows that death is near at hand.''

''That is all theorizing,'' said the banker, '' have you any proofs that your theory is correct ; that the prosperity of a people holds any relation to the amount of the cir_ culating medium?''

''The proof,'' said the other, '' is the present condition of the United States as compared with the condition in 1865, just thirty years ago. But if you need further proof I can refer you to all the great thinkers of the world who have ever written upon the subject. The famous Scotch historian, David Hume, a man whose opinions are received to-day with universal respect, said:

'' 'Falling prices, misery and destitution are inseparable companions. The disasters of the Dark Ages were caused by decreasing money and falling prices, With the increase of money, labor and industry gain new life.'

''The United States Monetary Commission, created August 15, 1876, made a report March 2, 1877, in which they said:

'' 'That the disasters of the Dark Ages were caused by decreasing money and falling prices, and that the recovery therefrom and the comparative prosperity which followed the discovery of America were due to an increasing supply of the precious metals and rising prices, will not seem surprising or unreasonable when the noble functions of money are considered. Money is the great instrument of association, the very fiber of social organism, the vitalizing force of industry, the protoplasm of civilization and as essential to its existence as oxygen is to animal life. Without money civilization could not have had a beginning, and with a diminishing supply it must languish, and. unless relieved finally perish.'

''The historian Allison states that when Christ was born there was $1,600,000,000 of gold and silver in the

Roman Empire, derived largely from the mines of Spain. But these mines became exhausted. The supply diminished ; the usurer plied his arts and the capitalist grasped the real estate ; all wealth was concentrated in a few hands, just as it is becoming to-day ; and the multitude were reduced to the lowest limit of degradation and wretchedness. They had no longer the courage or the public spirit of their forefathers, to defend their homes. And when a great white race, which had been nurtured in the storms and snows and ice of the remote north, a barbarous but noble people, schooled by suffering into heroism, a race of warriors and freemen, moved southward, toward the sun, and fell upon the imbecile aristocrats and degraded commonwealth of Rome, the mighty empire, once mistress of the known world, tumbled into a heap of ashes and was no more.

" But as culture increased among the conquerors and the distinctions of society arose, the rich desired the luxuries of the orient ; and, as they had nothing except the precious metals which the Hindoos wanted, in exchange for their silks and satins, and spices and jewels, the gold and silver had to go, by the slow moving caravans, from Europe to Asia never to return. We are told that a gold coin loses one-thirteen-hundredth part of its weight every year. Hence in thirteen hundred years it would all be dissipated. From these conjoined causes it came to pass that by the ninth century (as Allison tells us) the supply of gold and silver, of the countries embraced in the former Roman empire, had decreased from $1,600,000,000 to $150,000,000, or less than one dollar in ten! And as the coins became scarcer their exchangeable value necessarily increased, until a penny would buy a laborer's wages for a day, and two pence would buy a sheep or a bushel of wheat.

"We had what they call the Dark Ages. One writer observes: 'For a thousand years the mind of man made not a single step in advance.' A pall of desolation settled down on the human family. The very intellect of the race became torpid. But for the religious houses the arts of reading and writing would have disappeared, the alphabet have been lost, and civilization itself have perished in a black and sunless sea of barbarism. There were no wits, no poets, no historians, no orators for hundreds of years. The human race was practically dead."

"But," said Mr. Hutchinson, "did not the art of printing lift up the human family?"

"The art of printing," replied Mr. Sanders, "was a noble invention, (or importation), and in these latter ages has worked tremendous results, but of what use was a process to make books to a man whose wages were a penny a day? No. The 'renaissance,'—the resurrection of the human mind—was due to the increased supply of money in Europe, and the consequent increased activity in commerce, and the increased wealth. It

> "'Put a spirit of life in everything,
> Till jocund Nature laughed and leaped with it.'

"The time had come when He who made man perceived that he was traveling towards an abyss; and so He put it into the mind of an Italian adventurer to sail west to find India, and make a fortune out of pepper. His chief difficulty was that, in consequence of the rotundity of the globe, he believed he was going down hill as he went westward; that was simple enough; but how would

he ever climb that watery hill to get back to Spain?
There was the rub! But God makes use of blind instruments to do his greatest work; and so this geographer,
who believed that the East Indies lay where the West
Indies are, and that the globe was shrunken by the whole
width of the Pacific ocean, and who, in Cuba, sent an
embassy to wait on the Grand Kahn, became the means
by which the American continents were opened to overflowing Europe, and the gold and silver of Central
America, Mexico and Peru were torn from the walls of
the temples and converted into coin to lift up the
white race to the splendid development it has since
attained.

" This it was that made the printing press available;
this breathed immense and potent life into the alphabet;
this made art triumphant, for there was something with
which to buy its productions; this warmed the genius of
humanity into activity until Bacon, Cervantes, Mon-
taigne and a thousand others came to adorn the pages of
history. The increased supply of money, thus obtained,
was supplemented by the creation of bank credit. This,
like nearly all the great inventions or discoveries of value
to mankind, was stumbled upon. In 1171 the city of
Venice seized upon the wealth of its most opulent citizens
by a forced loan; it kept the money and gave the owners
credit upon its books; and these credits could never be
withdrawn, but were transferable at the pleasure of the
owners upon the books. They became of more value
than coins of like amounts, and rose to a premium, because the coins were worn and chipped and of uncertain
values. The system endured, with universal approval,
for 626 years. It practically doubled the volume of the
money which entered it, for the credit was the shadow of

the coin. In the seventeenth century similar banking
systems spread over Holland, Spain, France, England
and Italy, having the effect to still farther increase the
apparent volume of money and swell the growing flood
of civilization, until it has reached its present enormous
proportions.

URBAN AND RURAL INTELLIGENCE.

"You seem, sir," said Mr. Hutchinson, "to have stud-
ied the financial question very thoroughly."

"I fear there is a covert sneer in what you say,"
replied Mr. Sanders, "for the business men of the cities
usually feel that to be an agriculturist is to be a kind of
serf and ignoramus. But this is an unjust conclusion.
To handle money is not necessarily to know anything
about the great laws of finance. The merchant's whole
art is to buy at wholesale and sell at retail; to know his
customers and to be keen and quick in lookingafter his
collections. What is there in this that would give him
any right to speak on great economic questions? The
tanner or the shoemaker, because they deal in hides,
might just as well pretend to teach ex-cathedra as to
the raising of cattle or the treatment of their diseases.
The business man of the cities is absorbed in an infinite
number of petty details of trade; and if he has anytime
left, the theater, the concert hall, the club room, or the
lecture hall call him away. On the contrary, the farmer
is denied all these temptations to fritter away his time,
and is forced to think and study. The city man reads
the newspapers by glimpses at the headlines, snatched on
the street cars; the farmer devours the whole publication,
down even to the editorials. Hence it is a curious fact
that you can take hap-hazard a dozen intelligent country

residents and a like number of the inhabitants of the
cities, and let them discuss the financial issues of the day,
and it will be seen that the former are better informed
as to the monetary history of our country than the latter.
Thus it comes that the agricultural societies two or
three years ago were discussing the questions which
have only just now reached the horizon of the urban
population.

"The banker is an accumulator; he has the squirrel's
instinct to gather nuts; his mind is usually devoid of any
thought but a vehement desire to obtain riches.   He
knows the financial standing of every man who deals
with him, and he rates each one, not by his knowledge
of his virtue or his character, but by his bank account.
His maxim is, 'D——n your reputation; take care of
your credit.'   A Dunn or Bradstreet report is his Bible—
his encyclopædia—and he studies it with rapt devotion.
But you might just as well expect the nut-gathering
squirrel to give (if he could speak) some valuable suggestions to Linneus or Darwin, as to the relations of the
Rodentia to the rest of the animal kingdom, as to suppose that mere money-lenders would know anything
about statesmanship or the government of nations.   The
squirrel could tell the philosophers how best to climb a
tree with a nut in one's mouth, or how to recognize a
worm-hole; that is all.   The money-lender is profoundly
keen in finding out how much of a mortgage is on a
neighbor's house, or how much the fellow around the
corner, who owns a junk shop, is in debt.   But what
has that got to do with the great philanthropic purposes
which lie at the base of civilization?   And how can a
man whose life has been spent in concentrating the wealth
of the many into the pockets of the few, so conduct the

affairs of government that the inordinate greed of the
great plunderers of the world shall be restrained and the
many be lifted up to happiness ? "

" Do you mean to say that an inhabitant of a city cannot form correct conclusions on public affairs?" asked Mr.
Hutchinson.

" Not at all," replied the other, "some of the most
benevolent hearts and clearest brains in the world have
come from cities.   What I am trying to make plain is,
that money-lending is not a proper preparation for statesmanship ; and that mere success in nut-gathering does
not imply capacity for governing.   Now-a-days our cra-
ven-spirited people are down on their knees before the
millionaires, and asking them to rule the land ; and they
are nothing loathe to do so.   Indeed, as their criterion is
the bank account, they naturally push themselves forward and are striving to change our government from a
republic of equality to an oligarchy of wealth, and they
are rapidly accomplishing their purpose.   Only the shell
of liberty remains to-day."

THE AGGRESSIVENESS OF THE COURTS.

" Really, my dear sir," said Mr. Hutchinson, " I have
listened to you with a great deal of interest, because you
seem to have positive convictions so different from my
own conclusions, but when you say that only the shell of
liberty remains in the republic of the United States, you
say that which, (pardon me) seems to me absurd.   Where
can you find more liberty than there is in this country?
You can speak and print whatever you please ; you can
denounce the government as you are now doing, with im-
punity ; and you can vote as you please, for whomsoever
and whatsoever you please.   Where can you find greater
liberty than that?"

"All that appears to be true," replied Mr. Sanders, "but let us look a little into it.

"It is true that I can vote as I please, but what use is it for me to elect legislators to pass laws, which I may desire, when great corporations stand ready to buy them up to vote for laws which will oppress and impoverish me?"

"Well, you can agitate and expose the wrongs and unite the people to reform abuses. No corporations can stand up against a united public opinion."

"Very true; but how am I to reach the ears of the multitude? The great newspapers control them, and 'the money-power controls the newspapers.' I have to fall back on pamphlets or journals of limited circulation, or my own voice. And every argument I present is met by millions of printed lies so plausible, so ingenious, that only an expert can answer them; and by the time I have swept away one falsehood, a hundred more, like the heads of a hydra, spring up in its place. The ingenuity of falsification is something unparalled and appalling. The past history of the world, as I have said, furnishes nothing like it. What we call popular ignorance is simply universal newspaper deception."

"Well, my dear sir," said the banker, "if the wrongs of the people are real and not imaginary they will yet arise in their wrath and elect legislators and congressmen that will beat down the corruptionists and give the people good laws."

"Yes, sir," replied the other, "such a spasm of virtuous indignation, springing from the bosom of poverty and oppression, is possible, but then arises a darker danger."

"What is that?"

"You will agree with me that whatever makes the laws for the government of the people," said Mr. Sanders, "is the ultimate power in the land."

"Certainly," replied Mr. Hutchinson.

'And I think you will further agree with me that a power which can take the laws after they are passed, and say:—'this shall stand—but this shall not,' is higher than the power which makes the laws."

"Certainly," replied Mr. Hutchinson, "you refer to the veto of the president, I suppose."

"Not at all," replied Mr. Sanders, "that is all right ; it is provided for in the constitution ; it is part of the fundamental law. And the power at last rests with the people, through their senators and representatives. They can over-ride the president's veto and make a law in spite of the executive. But the power I refer to decides what shall be law and what shall not be law, and there is no appeal, under heaven, from its decision."

"I don't understand you."

"That power is the United States Supreme Court in the nation, and the local supreme courts in the states."

"Oh, that's all right," replied Mr. Hutchinson, "they are given that power in the national and state constitutions. They have the right to declare any law unconstitutional. I did not know what you were driving at."

"Well," said the other, taking a book out of his valise, "here is the constitution of the United States. Just look it over and point out the passage which gives the Supreme Court the power to over-ride congress and wipe out its laws. It is a brief document and it will take you but a few minutes to read it."

After a pause Mr. Hutchinson replied:

"I am very much surprised ; there is nothing here of the kind."

"Precisely," said the other. "On the contrary you will find that the opening words of the constitution are as follows:

"'Sec. I (Art. I.) All legislative powers herein granted shall be vested in a Congress of the United States, which shall consist of a Senate and a House of Representatives.'

"There is no proviso here—'subject to the approval of the Supreme Court of the United States.'

"If the framers of the constitution had intended that the Supreme Court had the right to amend an act of Congress, by striking out part and approving of another part, all of which are legislative functions, they would clearly have said so. Sec. 2 of Article III prescribes the limitation of the judicial powers, naming the different parties to actions, as controversies between two or more states, between a state and the citizens of another state, between citizens of different states, etc.; but it no where provides for bringing the United States or Congress before the court to test the validity of its laws. In fact so jealous were the people of the encroachments of an irresponsible judiciary that the same generation which adopted the constitution adopted an amendment to it, the XI, March 5, 1794, providing:

"'The judicial power of the United States shall not be construed to extend to any suit at law or equity, commenced or prosecuted against one of the United States, by citizens of another State, or by citizens or subjects of any foreign State.'

"If the constitution thus inhibits the dragging of a State into court, in the instances referred to, can it be pretended that it contemplates establishing a power in the Supreme Court to pass a wet sponge over all the enactments of Congress, or over any one act; and that it nevertheless nowhere clearly asserts that right in the letter of the constitution. The fact is that Thomas Jefferson, third president of the United States, author of the Declaration of Independence, and the greatest statesman the soil of America has produced, declared, until the hour of his death, that the Supreme Court had no such power to over-ride Congress; and it was indeed twelve years before the court dared to assume such a power; and then it was done by Chief Justice Marshall, as a part of the Hamiltonian programme to turn the republic into an aristocracy, looking to an eventual monarchy."

"But," said Mr. Hutchinson, "may not the Congress violate the direct letter of the constitution, and is it not necessary that a restraining power should exist somewhere?"

"True it is," said the farmer, "that ultimate and absolute power must, in the last resort, be lodged somewhere; and such power implies the right to make mistakes; but where can it be so safely lodged as in the Congress of the United States, which is merely the mouth-piece of the entire people? Every two years the popular branch of Congress has to go back to the people, for endorsement or repudiation; and, if they have made mistakes or transcended the limitations of the constitution, there the mistakes can be corrected and the offenders punished. But on the other hand the Supreme Court is composed of a few men holding their places for life, with no power of appeal to anything above them. In England, if a court does wrong, there remains the right to go into the House of Lords, to seek a revision of the erroneous judgment, but the House of Lords is part of the *legislative* department, and not the judicial."

"But," said the banker, "can not the Supreme Court of England set aside an act of Parliament as unconstitutional?"

"Certainly not.   Nothing of the kind was ever heard of or dreamed of.   Englishmen would rise in revolution against any proposition to place the whole power of deciding what laws should govern them in the hands of a dozen lawyers selected by the crown.   The queen herself, during her whole reign, has never dared to veto any act of Parliament demanded by the people.   Her dynasty would not endure twenty-four hours if she did, and she knows it.   The English people have not the craven spirit which has been indoctrinated into our own people by the plutocracy, through a servile daily press.   Parliament is

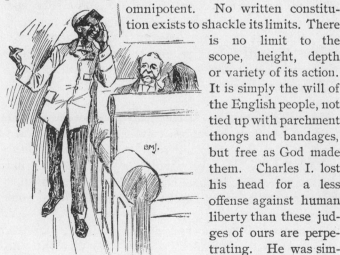

"*Dinner ready in the dining car.*"

omnipotent.   No written constitution exists to shackle its limits.   There is no limit to the scope, height, depth or variety of its action. It is simply the will of the English people, not tied up with parchment thongs and bandages, but free as God made them.   Charles I. lost his head for a less offense against human liberty than these judges of ours are perpetrating.   He was simply defending certain ancient prerogatives of the Executive.   He never pretended that he could take the statute books of England

and tear out all laws that did not meet with his approval.
They would have burned him alive at the stake if he had
attempted it."

"Dinner reaqy in the dining car," cried the porter.

"Let us get something to eat," said Mr. Hutchinson,
"and while I am eating I will digest your novel views."

*   *   *   *   *   *

"Mr. Sanders," said the banker, "your reasoning has
staggered me. I am surprised that I never saw anything
of the kind in our Chicago papers. They ransack the
heavens and the earth, the past, the present and the
future, to get material to fill up with. Strange that
they have never discussed this important question."

"Not at all," replied the other. "Talleyrand said the
object of language was to conceal one's thoughts; and
there are certain subjects which the daily press is pledged
to suppress. It is a vast conspiracy against the human
species; and types, ink and paper do the work better
than any other agency ever invented by the wit of man.
The conditions we live in are phenomenal, unprece-
dented."

"But seriously, Mr. Sanders, do you not think that
if the constitution prescribes certain limitations on the
power of Congress, as that it shall not pass an *ex post facto*
law, and Congress does pass such a law, that there should
be some power able to come in and say you have violated
the express terms of the constitution, and therefore your
law is null and void?"

"That would appear reasonable," said the farmer,
"but here is the difficulty: If you give the court the
power to over-ride Congress in a case of flagrant violation
of the express terms of the constitution, may it not assert
the same power as to cases less flagrant, and again, as to

cases less flagrant still ?   And having covered the ground
as to infringements of the *letter* of the constitution, will it
not advance to the question of violation of the *spirit* of
the constitution; and from this will it not go forward, (as
the Supreme Court did the other day in the income tax
decision), to consider what was the understanding or
expectation of some person or persons, named or un-
named, at the time of the adoption of the constitution or
thereabouts.   And thus the whole instrument will become
as clay in the hands of a potter, to fashion it into a pip-
kin, or, perchance, a crown, if you please.

*Uncle Sam.—"Get out of this, you infernal scamps!   You have turned my republic into
a moneyed oligarchy.   Out of my sight!   You are enemies of mankind!"*

"Why, in that income tax decision the court actually
proceeded so far as to amend the act of Congress by striking out a section here, and another there.   They can
go but one step farther, to-wit: To interpolate a few
lines in this place or that to make the statute agree with
what they think it should be."

"But you must admit," said Mr. Hutchinson, "that our judges of the Supreme Court are eminent and honorable men, and profound jurists."

"I admit nothing of the kind," was the reply. "Most of them were obscure men, never heard of, outside their own bailiwick, until they were elevated to the bench; and many of them earned the appointment by slavish servility to the cause of the corporations. The heroes of 1776, who made the revolution against the government of the English Parliament, of 600 members, never intended that the absolute and ultimate power of this nation should pass into the hands of nine men. There are no nine men on this round globe fit for such a gigantic trust. God never created them. If there are such, then a republican form of government is based upon a delusion and a snare."

"And the most threatening part of this business," continued Mr. Sanders, "is that these unauthorized judicial aggressions have gone on side by side with twenty other developments of the same kind, in the same direction, all looking to the enslavement of the American people."

THE PRESENT PER CAPITA OF CURRENCY.

"What are they?" asked the banker.

"I started yesterday to tell you how the present *per capita* of currency contrasts with that which we had in 1865 when it was $67.$\frac{20}{100}$."

"Yes; I should be glad to hear you farther on that subject," said Mr. Hutchinson. "We have now about $24 *per capita*, and that seems to me ample for all the business needs of this country."

"First let me call your attention," said Mr. Sanders, "to the effect of an abundant currency upon the condition

of the people. I quote from a hostile authority, from
a man who did as much harm to this country as any man
that ever lived—excepting John Sherman! I refer to
the Indiana banker, the War Secretary of the Treasury.
In his Report to Congress in 1865 he said:

" ' The country as a whole, notwithstanding the ravages of war, and the draft upon labor, is, by its greatly
developed resources, far in advance of what it was in 1857.

Citizen:—"If there is $25.00 per capita in
circulation I wonder where it is."
Money Lender:—"I know."

The people are now com-
paratively free from debt.
* * * There is an im-
mense volume of paper
money in circulation. *
* * Trade is carried
on more largely for cash
than ever was the case
previous to 1861, and
there is a much greater
demand for money than
there would be if sales
were made, as hereto-
fore, on credit. * * *
So far as individual in-
debtedness is regarded,
it may be remarked that the people of the United States
are much less in debt than in previous years.'

" What a charming picture of an earthly paradise is
here presented? The people free from debt. Business
on a cash basis. No land mortgages. No chattel mortgages. No one running to the banks to borrow money.
Nobody being devoured by interest charges. The land
smiling like a garden; the people happy; immigration

sweeping over new territories, displacing the prowling savages, opening fields, building homes, making the wilderness to blossom as the rose, marrying and giving in marriage, and creating new and mighty common-wealths. A million soldiers were discharged after that last grand review. The London *Times* said that the real test of our institutions was at hand; that those million armed men, fresh from scenes of carnage, would inaugurate a reign of rapine and violence from the Atlantic to the Pacific. I much fear that if they were turned loose to-day Coxey's army, marching to Washington, would return, drawing cannon and blazing with the fire of rifles. Then they were absorbed into the body of the people, who greedily welcomed them. They went to work at once. Not one of them became a 'tramp.' Never was there seen in the world such billing and cooing and love-making and nest-building as took place when these stalwart heroes selected mates and homes and settled down to share in the happiness of a universally prosperous people.

"But in the general rejoicing there was one class that was unhappy—the money-lenders. Mankind, for the first time in the history of the world, had escaped from their clutches. Nobody wanted their money. Every one had money of his own. Business was on a cash basis, prices were good, and everybody at work. They stood scowling at this magnificent picture of human develop-ment and happiness, like the devil looking in through the half-opened door of heaven.

"'This thing,' they said, 'must be stopped. Ruin must reform this over-abundant prosperity. We must draw the world back into the whirlpool of our manipula-tions.' And so they clamored around the Secretary of the Treasury at that time. And in the same report in which he painted the magnificent condition of the people, out of debt and uniformly prosperous, he urged that the devil must be turned loose in Paradise. He said:

"'There is an immense volume of paper money in circulation *which must be contracted.'*

"Ah! there sounded the funeral bell, ringing loud and terrible in the midst of the singing, shouting, hilarious holiday. But the merry roysterers took no notice of it. Little did they think that it was the clangor of doom. That it meant embarrassment, poverty, foreclosure, the desolation of homes; sin, death, crime; the bankruptcy of whole communities and unparalleled individual suffering. Little did they know that it summoned the sailor to desert the ship in the harbor, until its rotting sails dropped piecemeal on the moss-grown deck. Little did the frontierman understand that it was the bugle call to turn back from the wilderness, for the great march of triumphant civilization had halted.

"And what excuse was there for destroying a condition in which every one was prosperous. Here we have it in that same report of the Secretary:

"'The expansion has now reached such a point as to be absolutely oppressive to a large portion of the people, while, at the same time, it is diminishing labor, and is *becoming subversive of good morals.* * * * There is no fact more manifest, than that the plethora of money is undermining the morals of the people by encouraging waste and extravagance.'

"Think of that! Think of this cold-hearted Secretary putting such lies into his official report! The good times were 'absolutely oppressive to a large portion of the people.' Who were they? Not the farmers; for they were getting $1.50 per bushel for their wheat, and everything else in proportion. Not the miners or manufacturers, for the output of mills and mines could not keep up with the demand. Not the body of the people, for they were, the Secretary has just told us, generally out of debt—an unprecedented condition. What class is left? The money-lenders. These are the ones who seize upon the medium of exchange, provided by the government for the convenience of the whole population, and monopolize it, and lend it out on terms and conditions that force their fellow men to work for them, while they fatten in idleness. These were the men to whom the good times and the universal prosperity were 'absolutely oppressive.'

"It is true that the Secretary tries to hide the money-lending class behind the workingmen. He says the abundant supply of money is "diminishing labor." This is false upon its face; for in the same report he says, 'There is a larger demand than formerly for money on the part of manufacturers for the payment of operatives." Think of that. Labor was diminished by the good times! But the

manufacturers needed more money to pay their hands.
And Mr. Justice Bradley, of the Supreme Court, said:

" 'It is an undoubted fact, that during the late civil
war the activity of the workshops and factories, mines and
machinery, shipyards, railroads and canals of the loyal
states, *caused by the issue of legal-tender currency*, consti-
tuted an inexhaustible fountain of strength to the national
cause.'

"Here we have the employment of labor, and the consequent prosperity of the country, traced to an abundant
legal-tender currency; but this Benedict Arnold, McCulloch, at whose doorstep lie the bodies of an infinite
number of bankrupts, paupers, murderers, suicides, aban-
doned women and starving tramps; this man, I say, while
perfectly aware that an abundant currency sets all the
wheels of commerce, trade and labor in motion, had the
effrontery to declare that the abundance of money and
prosperity "diminished labor;" and in the name of labor
he turned labor out to starve.

"Oh it is simply horrible.

DISQUALIFYING BANKERS.

"If Ralph Izard, Senator from South Carolina, had not
changed his vote, on Thursday, Jan. 16th, 1794 (see
Benton's Abridg't of Debates in Congress, Vol. 1, p.
446), McCulloch, the Indiana banker, never would have
been Secretary of the Treasury to sacrifice the happiness
of the American people."

"How is that?" enquired Mr. Hutchinson.

"It was at that time," said Mr. Sanders, "that Congress
was at work formulating amendments to the newly
adopted constitution. It was then the amendment was
adopted and submitted to the people, to which I have
already referred, limiting the power to sue a state. On
December 24, 1793 (p. 445 *ibid*), we read:

" '*Exclusion of bank officers and stockholders from Congress.*

"The following motion was made and seconded, to-wit: 'That the constitution be amended by adding, at the end of the ninth section of the first article, the following clause:

'Nor shall any person holding any office or stock in any institution in the nature of a bank for issuing or discounting bills or notes payable to bearer or order, under the authority of the United States, be a member of either house whilst he holds such office or stock, but no power to grant any charter of incorporation, or any commercial or other monopoly, shall be herein implied.'

" 'And it was agreed that this motion should lie for consideration.'

"And on Thursday, January 16, 1794, it came up again and an amendment was offered that no 'person holding any office in the Bank of the United States' should ' be a member of either House while he holds such office.' *This was adopted by a vote of 13 yeas and 12 nays.* But the question coming up again, on the same day, Mr. Izard, of South Carolina, changed his vote, and it was lost; yeas 12, nays 13; and thereupon the matter seems to have been dropped. If Mr. Izard had not changed his vote this amendment to the constitution would have been adopted; and that the people would have ratified it there can be no doubt. If this had been done it would have become part of the fundamental law of this nation that bankers were not fit persons for the execution of public trusts, and the country would have been saved great suffering and misgovernment."

"That is rather hard on my profession," said Mr. Hutchinson.

" It is and it is not. There was a time when the Christian world permitted none but Jews to lend money for profit, and this was done because the Jews, it was understood—as an accursed generation—were going to the devil anyhow, and a little superfluity of sin, more or less, could not make much difference to them. When a man is damned (they thought), he is at the end of his rope, and the difference in temperature of different parts of Satan's kingdom is something for self-registering thermometers, and not a matter to be considered by ordinary philosophers.

" But statesmanship has, for its basis, charity, kindliness, philanthropy. The cast of mind that is required is diametrically opposite from that of the man who contemplates his fellow creatures as subjects to be slaughtered, stripped and devoured. In the former the magnetic needle of purpose points directly away from the pole of selfishness to the universal good; in the latter case all the needles concentrate on *self*—dipping down, perchance, to the grave and rottenness and oblivion. And yet we are not to feel incensed against the nut-gathering tribe. It is their instinct. They can no more help the cast of their minds than they can the cast of their features, and one generally fits the other. They are performing a part in the universal panorama. But while the many are required to accumulate, to a few in every generation is given the serious and thankless task of trying to protect humanity from itself; and they can no more help their philanthropy than the others can help their greediness. The Man-Behind-the-Scenes takes charge of all that, and He knows what He is about. So while we strive to lift up humanity (for that, too, is part of God's purpose), let us have all charity for the forest-prowlers, the tigers, wolves and jackals, who cannot, by any exercise of will or conscience, be anything but tigers, wolves and jackals to the end of the chapter. It is our duty to our wives and little ones that we keep the beasts in the bushes and not permit them to ravage the world and devour the babies. A wise philanthropy must resist a brutal and destructive selfishness, which will take to-morrow what it cannot carry away to-day, and will continue to prey until the whole land is a desolate wilderness. The instinct to grab is like all other instincts—insatiable and unreasonable. Go talk to the bacilli of consumption, swarming in every fiber of the victim's body, and tell them that if they continue to breed and eat the man must surely die, and 'the barren rage of death's eternal cold' will settle down upon them in the silent grave. Will they stop? It is impossible. Go tell the money-grabbers that they are producing universal ruin, and that at last their victims will rise up and crush them, perhaps amid the horrors of anarchy —with reeking sword and flaming torch. Will they stop? No more than the bacilli. They cannot. They are the slaves of their instinct.

UNDERMINING THE MORALS.

"But let me return to that declaration of the Secretary of the Treasury, in 1865, that the currency must be contracted because the general prosperity was 'undermining the morals of the people.'

"Great God! That all the horrors of the last thirty years should be inflicted on the people in the name of Morality!! That men should be denied work; evicted from their homes; forced to eat the bitter bread of charity; families separated; girls driven to lives of shame; men enforced to violence and crime or suicide; millions compelled to become tramps, wretched half-fed nomads and barbarians; the whole peaceful, orderly and beautiful face

·of society changed to the scowling countenance of universal apprehension, distrust and danger! And all this brought on the land—in the name of MORALITY—by a lying, hypocritical banker, fresh from his shaving-shop in Indiana.

"'Morality!' Why this rascal knew perfectly well that sin is, in nine cases out of ten, the bloody sweat of want; that idleness is the devil's chief agency to achieve evil; that the empty sack cannot stand upright, and that when he plunged this country into universal ruin, to please the money-lenders, he was placing dynamite under both morality and religion, and endangering the very coherence of human society.

"'Morality!' He should be whipped to death by a gang of murderers and bankrupts."

"Well, well," said Mr. Hutchinson, "give over your rage against Mr. McCulloch, who is a very respectable gentleman, and come back to the question of the present per capita of circulation."

"Pardon me," said the other, "if I let my temper run away with me. But such things are enough to

'' Breed a fever in the blood of age,
    And make an infant's sinew strong as steel.'

" You claimed that we had an abundant currency for all the needs of the country."

FRANCE AND THE UNITED STATES.

" Yes; about $25 per capita," said Mr. Hutchinson.

"Well, France has, according to some authorities, $50 per capita; according to others $45; none place it lower than $40. Why should the people of the United States have less money in circulation than the people of France? "

"The reason is plain," replied Mr. Hutchinson. "In this country a large part of our business is done by checks."

"But is there not, or ought there not to be, in every case the money to meet the checks?" said Mr. Sanders. "If a man draws a check without the money to meet it, you send him to prison. The check is no substitute for money; it simply facilitates the exchange or payment of money. But the use of checks is only another form of credit. If I take A. B.'s check for $1,000 and pay a debt with it to C. D., I do it because I have confidence in A. B. and C. D. has confidence in me. But the question arises, should the business of the country depend upon *credit*? Should it depend upon the solvency of individuals or banks, or their willingness to accommodate their customers?"

"But," replied Mr. Hutchinson, "the people do not need so much money in this country as they do in France."

"On the contrary," replied Mr. Sanders, "the annual crop of the United States amounts to billions of dollars, and every part of them, every bushel of wheat or corn or oats, and every pound of cotton, or beef or pork or mutton has to be paid for in cash. The producer has to have his pay in cash. Only in one instance that I ever heard of were checks used in the purchase of a crop from the farmers. That was a few years ago, when the millers of Minneapolis could not obtain the necessary currency—it was too scarce—and they bought wheat, through parts of the northwest, with their own checks on the banks of Minneapolis. But they were accepted with much grumbling by the farmers and merchants, and the practice soon ceased. But the fact shows not only that money is not abundant enough for the needs of the country, but that it is absolutely essential in quantities proportionate to the great crops we raise in the United States. Every year, when the crops are to be moved, the whole business of the country is disarranged by the withdrawal of currency from the great money centers to the west and south, and the dangerous strain is not relieved until the crops find their way to the seaboard. Why then, I repeat, should we have less money, per capita, in this country than they have in France? Ours is an expanding population, spreading over a vast continent, one of the greatest subdivisions of the earth's surface. France is a small country, comparatively; tucked away in one corner of Europe. Our line of frontier has been advancing for years forty miles each year from west and east. France has no colonies but a strip along the red-hot coast of Northern Africa. The United States increases in population about thirty per cent. every ten years. The French people scarcely increase in number at all. And yet we, you say, have $25 per capita, and France has about $45. Why? Why should we be chained down in this way when we have the right to supply ourselves with currency just as we do with postage stamps?

PAPER MONEY AND POSTAGE STAMPS.

"What would be said if the government printed only half as many postage stamps as were necessary, and thus put them at a premium? Would not the people rise up and drive the knaves and tricksters out of power who were guilty of such an act? And is there any more reason why a man should not be able to exchange anything he has to sell for money, than there is why he should not be able to obtain postage stamps for his correspondence?

There was a time, Hugh McCulloch tells us, when business in this country was conducted on a purely cash basis. Is not that the normal condition of things? Does not credit simply mean a deficiency of cash, which has put cash to a premium, equal to the interest the business man has to pay for its use?''

''But your comparison of money to postage stamps is fallacious,'' said Mr. Hutchinson.

''Why? Both represent the credit of the nation. The postage stamp is simply a little national note, with mucilage on its back. You take a national promissory note for $5, with green on its back, and the government receives it in exchange for 500 little national notes of one cent each, with gum on their backs. There is little or no intrinsic value in either. They represent the faith and credit of the nation, the wealth and power of 70,000,000 people. They are merely a function; they perform an office; they are universally accepted tokens; and as long as they do the work assigned them you enquire no farther. You never stop to ask the intrinsic value of the postage stamp. You know that it will carry your letter from Maine to Alaska—half around the globe. And what do you care about the intrinsic value of the $5 greenback? You know you can swap it for 500 one cent postage stamps, or you can take it to the custom house and pay $5 of duties on goods imported from abroad; or you can pay $5 of internal revenue taxes with it; or $5 of your income tax, and you know that your neighbor or your creditor will take it, not only because it is legal tender, but because he too can pay duties or taxes or purchase postage stamps or pay debts with it. It represents the consensus of resolve of 70,000,000 people.''

''But,'' said the other, ''you have got to pay money to

buy your postage stamps, and you folks propose to issue greenbacks by the wagon load, and give them away."

"We never proposed anything of the kind," said Mr, Sanders. "We do not propose to put forth a single dollar of paper money unless we get a full equivalent for it. If we owe A, B, C and D for services rendered as cabinet ministers, senators, congressmen, soldiers, sailors, officials of all kinds from judges to tide-waiters, and we hand them out an amount of greenbacks equal to the sums we owe them, certainly no one has the right to complain that there has not been a full and adequate consideration for those notes. Your people, on the contrary, propose to take the faith and credit of the United States, which we chopped up into little non-interest-bearing obligations of $5 or $10 each, and put it forth in the shape of larger notes, for $1,000 or $10,000 each, called "bonds," bearing interest, and you will furnish us with the chopped chicken-feed we call money, and take your pay in the interest on the bonds. Now we think the nation can cut up its credit into small bills, without cost, just as well as a few individuals called bankers can do it at large cost to the people, whose credit and legal-tender power is at the back of the transaction in either case."

"But," said Mr. Hutchinson, "the government is not fitted to go into the banking business."

"Just as much," said Mr. Sanders, "as the bankers are fitted to go into the governing business."

"But the government cannot receive money on deposit and discount merchants' notes and sell exchange, etc."

"Not at all. It never pretended to. That is legitimately a banking business and is properly left in the hands of private individuals. But that is not the question at issue. The question is, who is to create the money with which that banking business is to be carried on—the banks or the people, acting through their government? In all nations the gold and silver and copper and nickel coins have, during all ages, been minted and stamped and endowed with the properties of money by the government. No nation ever turned this power over to individuals. No private parties ever ran a mint."

"I remember," said Mr. Hutchinson, "one instance where the power to coin money was delegated to a private party. In 1724 the English government conferred on one Wood a royal grant, authorizing him to coin £108,000 in half-pence and farthings, for circulation in Ireland."

"True; and Dean Swift attacked the project in his celebrated 'Drapier's Letters,' and the people refused to take Wood's money, and he was ruined. Walpole threatened to arrest Swift, but he was told that it would require an army of 10,000 men to take him, and that a revolution would follow. So you see the exception you have quoted proves the rule. And the fact remains, that the bankers of the United States have never claimed the right to coin gold or silver or copper or nickel pieces; but they do claim the right to put forth paper money. Now what is the difference between them? Gold and silver are not money until stamped with the government stamp. They are commodities."

"But," said Mr. Hutchinson, "you can take $1,000 of gold bullion and pay a debt with it anywhere in the world."

"Yes; if your creditor is willing to accept it. But you can do the same with $1,000 of wheat or potatoes. But you cannot force any one to take any kind of commodity unless he chooses to do so. They are not legal tender. The leg.l tender quality is affixed by the government alone, and that to which it is affixed is money and nothing else is.''

"But our gold coins circulate abroad," said Mr. Hutchinson, "they are good on both sides of the Atlantic."

"No; you are wrong. You will see no more American coin in England than you will see English coin in America, and when has the private citizen here received an English sovereign in the course of business? When you make a trip abroad you buy drafts on London, Paris, Berlin, etc., and if you have any American money in your pocket when you go aboard the steamer, you go to the purser and he gives you English money in exchange for it."

"But you must admit that if you found yourself in London with a pocket full of American gold coin you could go to the first bank and sell them for English money."

"Yes," replied Mr. Sanders, "but you sell it as a commodity, just as you could sell 1,000 bushels of American wheat in a Liverpool granary. You can get the market price for it."

"But the market price of gold is uniform," replied Mr. Hutchinson.

"Not at all. According to the highest financial authorities in Europe, the price of gold has increased 33 per cent. in the last twenty years, as measured by the value of anything and everything else."

"Well," said Mr. Hutchinson, "you must admit then that it is reliable."

"Yes; at the expense of all other commodities; at the expense of human labor and its productions; at the expense of human life and happiness and virtue; at the expense of religion and liberty and everything this earth holds precious.

"'Let's shut our gates and sleep; manhood and honor
Should have hare-hearts; would they but fat their thoughts
With this crammed metal.'

"All the ancient legends of mankind tell of a dragon which once devoured the sun, the moon, the stars and the earth—the Leviathan, the Midgard-serpent, the Dog-Garm, the Fenris-wolf, Seb, Typhon, Lucifer, Set, Satan, the principle of evil in the universe. The Fiery Dragon has broken loose again on the orderly affairs of this

world, and is devouring our globe, with all its glories, interests and beauties."

"But you have not yet shown me," said the banker, "what is the real per capita of money in circulation in the United States. Let us leave the Fiery Dragons alone for a while and come down to practical details."

"Pardon me for wandering off," replied Mr. Sanders, "but this is so vast a subject, and so obscured by misunderstandings and misrepresentations, that it is difficult to treat it like a proposition in Euclid.

THE TRUE PER CAPITA.

"Let me see," continued Mr. Sanders. "You claim that there are about $25 in circulation for every man.

woman and child in the United States. I shall try to demonstrate that there is much less.

"But, in the first place, I would say that the reports issued by the government of the United States are perfectly unreliable. They are a mass of lies."

"What!" cried Mr. Hutchinson, "you don't mean to say that the government itself puts forth false reports. Why, it is treason—sacrilege to say so. If we cannot believe our national officers, whom can we believe?"

"Well, I assert," replied Mr. Sanders, "that the reports put forth by the Treasury Department of the United States, at different times, as to the same matters, are utterly contradictory, and one or other of them must be outrageously false."

"I would like to see the proof of that," said the banker.

"Well, here you have it," replied Mr. Sanders, reading his figures from a little book he carried in his pocket.

"The ninth statistical abstract of the Treasury Department for 1885 gave certain statements to show the amount of money in circulation in the United States from 1857 to 1886; and six years afterwards the same Treasury Department made a similar statement as to the amount in circulation during the same years, and the difference between the two statements is so great that one would think they were surely issued by two different nations. Examine this table carefully and see how much government reports are to be depended upon:

Year.	9th Abstract Aggregate Circulation.	16th Abstract Aggregate Circulation.
1862	$ 532,832,079	$ 334,697,774
1864	1,062,840,516	669,441,478
1866	1,079,013,645	673,488,244
1870	934,423,019	675,212,794
1874	1,024,571,016	776,083,031
1886	1,747,331,525	1,252,700,555
Total	$6,481,010,800	$4,381,623,886

"Here, in six years, we find a difference in the reports of the same department of the same government as to the same years amounting to *over two billions of dollars!* Either one statement or the other is a base and absolute lie. The probability is that neither of them is to be depended upon. 'False in one thing,' says the old Latin maxim, 'false in all.' We find the solid earth giving away under our feet—temples and towers reel around us, when the agents of the greatest government on earth lie in that ghastly fashion. How can we build on any statement they put forth? How will we know that the books and accounts of the world's chief republic have not been 'doctored' by some nasty little clerk, in the interest of the money-power? Our faith is shaken in everything. But worse than all, the sixteenth abstract says that for the years 1865, 1866 and 1867 the money in circulation was, on an average, $683,394,436, while the Secretary of the Treasury, in his report for 1868, says that from September 1, 1865, to September 1, 1867, the currency was reduced by funding and destroying $797,725,317! So that the amount destroyed or withdrawn from circulation was $115,000,000 more than the average amount in circulation, and there was *therefore $115,000,000 less than nothing in the hands of the people!!* The question does not seem to have been: ' What were the facts?' but ' What kind of statements do the exigencies of the money-power require?' If it could be shown that there was a small amount of money in circulation in 1867, then it answered the contention that our ' hard times,' in 1895, were due to a contraction of the circulation; and so the government statistics become plastic in the hands of the government officials.

"On July 1st, 1893, the Secretary of the Treasury gave, in his official report, the total amount of money in circulation as $2,323,547,977—an immense sum—made up as follows:

Gold coin.	$519,156,102
Gold bullion.	78,541,583
Silver dollars.	419,332,450
Fractional silver coin.	78,415,123
Silver bullion.	119,113,911
Total coin and bullion.	$1,213,559,169
United States notes.	$346,681,016
Treasury notes, 1890.	147,190,227
National bank notes	178,713,872
Gold certificates.	94,041,189
Silver certificates.	330,956,504
Currency certificates.	12,405,000
Total paper currency.	$1,109,988,808
Aggregate	$2,323,547,977

" But the Secretary then admits that in the foregoing table he has not only counted in the gold and silver but the certificates put forth to represent them, thus doubling the amount. This is certainly an extraordinary performance. And thereupon the Secretary makes another table, and the circulation falls, at one swoop, from $2,-323,547,977 to $1,738,954,057—a falling off of more than half a billion dollars!

"Here are the revised figures:

Gold	$597,697,685
Silver	615,861,484
Notes	525,394,888
Total	$1,738,954,057

Or $584,593,923 less than the first figures given !

"And these revised figures are put forth by the Secretary of the Treasury as the amount of money in circulation among the people ! Mark you ! Among the people !

"And yet in this latter statement of 'effective money,' the secretary includes the following amounts of bullion—bars of uncoined metal—that could not circulate among the people any more than could the ore in the gold mines.

Gold bullion	$ 78,541,583
Silver bullion	119,113,911
	$197,655,494

"Let us deduct this amount of commodity from the revised table of circulation, $1,738,954,057, and we have left $1,541,298,563.

"But a large part of this is locked up in the treasury (see p. 17, Report Treasurer for 1893), viz.:

Gold coin	$96,519,888
Silver coin	25,636,899
Notes	19,950,496
Total	$142,107,283

'Surely that which is in the vaults of the treasury is not in circulation among the people   We will thererore deduct this sum, $142,107,228, from the revised statement, less the bullion, to-wit: $1,541,298,563, and we have left $1,399,191,335.

''But this is not all. The report on the finances for 1893 shows that there were 3781 national banks in that year, and they were by law required to hold a certain amount of money in their vaults as a reserve fund, not to be put out under any circumstances. So far as the use of this money among the people is concerned it might just as well be at the bottom of the Atlantic. On October 3, 1893, this 'reserve' amounted to $513,900,000. Deduct this again from the $1,399,191,335 and we have left $885,291,335.

''But this is not all. In 1893 there were in this country 5,685 state, savings, private banks, etc., which held $3,070,462,680 of deposits. The state laws require a reserve fund for the security of depositors; in some cases it is 10 per cent, in others 25 per cent. Put it at the lowest figure, 10 per cent, and the reserve thus withdrawn from circulation would amount to $307,046,268, which taken from the $885,281,335 leaves us as the real money in circulation $581,255,067.

''This is a tremendous shrinkage from the $2,323,547,-997 first given by the Secretary of the Treasury in his report for July 1st, 1893. It is down to less than one-fourth.

'' But even this is not all.

''The Secretary of the Treasury in that report for July 1, 1893, gave the amount of gold and gold bullion in circulation in the United States as $597,697,685. How did he get those figures? He took as his basis the amount of gold coin in the treasury of the United States and the national banks on June 30, 1872, to-wit: $115,000,000, and added to it the estimated total of gold in circulation, at that time, among the people of the whole country, $20,000,000, and thus obtained a total cf $135,000,000. To this he added all that had been coined at the mints since 1872, with the gain or loss of gold exported or imported, as registered at the custom houses, deducting $3,500,000 used each year in the industrial arts. As the total amount of gold used in the arts in the world every year is stated by high-authority to be about $80,000,000, the sum of $3,500,000 for the United States would seem to be altogether too small. There is no country where the teeth of the people appropriate so much gold as in the United States.

"But the Secretary of the Treasury presupposes that every dollar ever coined of gold or silver since 1873 is still in existence. This is absurd. In the first decade of the present century there was coined, in one year, 10,000 silver dollars; of these only half a dozen are in existence to-day, and these are in the cabinets of numismatists, and are worth hundreds of times their original value, as curios.

> " 'Time hath, my Lord, a wallet at his back,
> Wherein he puts alms for oblivion."

"How many millions of dollars were destroyed in the great Chicago fire, and in the thousands of other fires in this country since 1872? How many have gone down to the bottom of the ocean in the hundreds upon hundreds of shipwrecks? How many have been buried in the earth and lost forever?

"In the report on the production of gold and silver for 1888, page 42–43, we read:

" ' In years past we have often insisted that there must be an error in the item, because the most industrious inquiry failed to bring to light a very considerable portion of it.   At present there are at least $275,000,000 of the total (gold coin) *which cannot be accounted for."*

" It does not seem reasonable, if there are nearly $600,-000,000 of gold coin or bullion in this country, that the reserve of the United States Treasury of $100,000,000 should fall to half that amount ; and that the government seemed to think it could not replenish its vaults unless it contracted with the Rothschilds, across the ocean.   Surely if there had been $600,000,000 in the hands of the people of the United States, the government could have raised whatever it needed by a popular loan among our own people, without having recourse to foreigners.   The statement is an egregious falsehood, put forth to deceive the people, by making them believe that nearly $600,000,000 of gold is in circulation among them, while east and west, north and south, a gold coin is something rarely or never seen by the citizens of our country.   Let us, therefore, deduct $250,000,000 of non-existent gold from that gross total of circulation, $581,255,067 and we have left $331,255,067. But this is not all.   In his estimate the Secretary of the Treasury counted in $419,332,550 silver and $77,415,123 of silver coin, or $496,747,673, in all ; because that was the total amount of silver dollars and fractional silver coin minted from February 28, 1878, to November 1, 1893. Here again not a particle of deduction is made for the losses by fires, floods, shipwrecks or hoards buried and lost.   We would, I think, be justified in deducting ten per cent, or $49,674,767 ; but following a recent, clearheaded writer on this subject, we will call it $20,000,000 ; and deducting this from the $331,255,067 we have left $281,580,300.

" But we have not yet made any allowance for the *paper* money destroyed, or lost, or worn out.   There were several millions of the fractional paper currency which was never presented for reduction. None of it exists to-day out of the cabinets of the curious. Of the $1,779,685,355 of national bank notes, issued since 1863, $1,570,985,166 have been redeemed, and the remainder, $208,701,189, are probably lost.

" If, then, we deduct the ten per cent. for the wear and tear, fires and shipwrecks, etc., of the last thirty years, so far as relates to the national bank notes alone, upon the amount now claimed to be in circulation, $178,-713,872, and we have $17,871,387, which, deducted from the gross total of all money in circulation, leaves us $263,708,913.

" I could also deduct a percentage for losses on United States greenbacks but I have shown enough, I think, for my purpose."

" I should say so," replied Mr. Hutchinson. " I had to hold my breath as you proceeded. I began to fear you were going to whittle it all away."

" Well, is there anything I have claimed that is not reasonable and probably true ?" inquired Mr. Sanders.

"I cannot say as to that just now," was the reply. " I will have to copy your figures and look them over at my leisure. You certainly make some startling statements."

" Let us take these figures, said Mr. Sanders:

$263,708,913

as the real amount in circulation to-day, and inquire how much that is per capita.

" The total population of the United States, according to the census of 1890, was 62,622,250. Five years have elapsed since that census was taken; we are half way

through the decade. Our increase in population, since
the establishment of our government, has been at the
average rate of 30 per cent. for every ten years. But let
us call it for the present decade only 20 per cent. Then
the growth for five years would be 10 per cent., or 6,262,-
225. Add this to the figures shown by the census, and
our present population is at least 68,884,475 persons.
Now let us divide $263,708,913, the amount of money
actually in circulation, among the citizens of the republic,
by 68,884,475, and we have as the

Per capita circulation, 1893..........**$3.84**

"Here, then, we have the difference between 1865
and 1895:

1865, per capita.... ....**$67.26**
1895, " " **3.84**

"This is in thirty years.

"There is a story told about a venerable colored gentleman who went fishing along the bank of a creek, down
South. To his delight he caught a very large catfish.
Vi.... ... c.. grand banquet that night floated before his
min ..yc. But, like all mortals, he was unsatisfied; he
wanted more. He thought he would continue down the
stream and double his splendid luck, and bring joy into
the faded eyes of his aged partner. But it would not do
to carry his prize through the sunshine on his journey-
ings. He would keep it fresh and take it up on his return. And so, running a piece of twine through its gills,
he selected a deep, cool pool, and returned the fish to its
native element, tying the other end of the string to a
sapling. And then he departed in search of further con-
quests. He had not been gone long when a youngster of
his own complexion, intent on finny spoil, but not favored

by the gods, happened along. He had secured only a
very diminutive catfish by an afternoon's labor. He
caught sight of the string. He gently lifted it from the
water, and his eyes and mouth distended as he contemplated the splendid trophy pendant at the end of it. The
great poet has said:

> "Woman is not in her best moments strong,
> But want will perjure the ne'er-touched vestal.

"And if this be true of woman, as it doubtless is, it is
ten times more true of man, and twenty times more true
of undeveloped man, to wit: the boy of any complexion.
And so the young fisherman deftly removed the great
fish from the line and substituted his diminutive spoil in
its place. He doubtless thought (for poets simply express
the universal sentiments of the race):

> "'A fair exchange is no robbery,
> Much less pure charity.'

"And then he meandered away. In the mean time our
elderly friend fished on and on, but with poor success.
He was happily unconscious of the great wrong that had
been done him:

> "'He that is robbed, not wanting what is stolen,
> Let him not know't and he's not robbed at all.'

"And so, smiling over the anticipated supper, which
he already smelled in imagination, with all its crisp and
appetizing flavors, he came to the scene of the robbery.
He stooped and drew up the string.

> "'Horror on horror's head accumulate!'

"His eyes popped out. His hands moved ugly. At
last he spoke, looking around him the while:
"'Dis is de same place. Dis is de same poplar. Dis

" Gor-Amity !   How you hab shrunk !"

is de same string.   Dis *must* be de same fish.   *But—gor-amity how you hab shrunk.*'

"And when we look at those figures:

        1865, per capita. **$67.26**
        1895, "   " **3.84**

"We are ready to cry out, with our venerable colored friend:

"'Gor-amity how you hab shrunk!'

"And as the old gentleman's fish was stolen so has been our currency.   It was a deliberate conspiracy of the money-lending class.   They have wrecked the whole land for their own profit.   They did it deliberately; they did it with malice prepense and aforethought; it was the question of their profit against the happiness of the whole human family dwelling in this land.   Hugh McCulloch was their mouthpiece.   He said, in 1865, to Congress:

"'The first thing to be done is to establish the policy of contraction.'

"And the House of Representatives, December 18, 1865, adopted the following resolution:

"'Resolved, that this House cordially concurs in the views of the Secretary of the Treasury, in relation to the necessity of a contraction of the currency.'

"And on April 12, 1866, Congress passed a law to contract the currency (14 statutes at large, 31), which gave the Secretary of the Treasury the power, 'at his discretion, to receive any treasury notes, or other obligations issued under any act of Congress, whether bearing interest or not, in exchange for any description of bonds authorized by said act, either in the United States or elsewhere, to such an amount, in such manner and at such rates as he may think advisable ;   *   *   *   the proceeds thereof to be *used only for retiring treasury notes or other obligations* issued under any act of Congress.'

"And this was done because, said Mr. McCulloch, ' the people are now comparatively free of debt ; ' ' the people are much less in debt than in previous years;' 'the country is far in advance of what it was in 1857 ; ' and ' the plethora of money is *undermining the morals of the people ! !* '

"And this noble effort to preserve the morals of the people by reducing them to beggary, has continued with but little change or variation from that day to this, during *thirty years !*   And the great question before our people is *whether or not it shall continue through all the future !*

HOW THE CUURRENCY WAS REDUCED.

" Congress backing him up and the money-power of Europe and America anxious to get the bonds of the great Republic, the accomplished money-lender of Indiana progressed splendidly in the work of enslaving the American people.

"On pages 28-9, Messages and Documents, 1867-8, the Secretary of the Treasury, Hugh McCulloch, says:

"During the month of September, 1865, the army having been reduced to a peace footing, it became apparent that the internal revenues would be sufficient to pay all the expenses of the government and the interest on the public debt, so that thenceforward the efforts of the Secretary were to be turned from borrowing to funding. Thus the condition of the country and the treasury determined the policy of the Secretary, which has been to convert the interest bearing bonds, notes, etc., into gold bearing bonds, and to contract the paper circulation by the redemption of United States notes.   For the last two years this policy has been steadily but carefully pursued and the result on the whole has been satisfactory to the Secretary.

"From the 1st of September, 1865, to the 1st of September, 1867, the Secretary says the 'reduction in the currency was as follows:

Compound interest notes were reduced from............	$217,024,160.00 to	$ 72,875,040.00
Seven and three-tenth notes were reduced from.......	830,000,000.00 to	337,978,800.00
United States notes and fractional currency from. ...	459,505,311.51 to	387,871,487.39

A reduction of........................$797,725,317.30

and the cash in the treasury has been increased from $88,215,055.13 to $133,998,398.02, and the funded debt has increased $686,584,800, while this has been accomplished there has been no commercial crisis and no considerable financial embarrassment.'

"'The Secretary continued,' says Bolles' Financial History, page 278, to 'reduce the legal tender notes, though not with regularity, and when Congress convened in December, a considerable stringency existed in the money market. The price of commodities had declined, and opposition to further contraction was loud and general,' and an 'act to suspend the further reduction of the currency,' became a law February 4, 1868 (15 Statutes at Large, 34).

"Think of that! The real money in circulation, according to McCulloch, on July 1st, 1865, was $2,113,-606,702.51, and of this $797,725,317.39, or more than one-third was wiped out of existence in two years!

"But we have talked the day away. There is the cry for supper—and that is, to the American, what the muzzin cry of the Mohammedan is to prayers—a summons that cannot be disobeyed."

"That is," said Mr. Hutchinson, "the American is as prompt in his eating as the mussulman is in his praying."

"Exactly," said Mr. Sanders, "and in this country the physical preponderates over the spiritual. Hence our inventions are multiplying and our religion decreasing."

THIRD DAY.

THE GOSPEL OF GREED.

"Good morning, Mr. Sanders. Are you too tired to talk this bright day?"

"Not at all; there are some themes I never tire of. I can say with Hamlet:

> "'Why, I will fight with him upon this theme,
> Until my eyelids do no longer wag.'

"Talk is words; but behind this discussion are tremendous things—the progress of development, the happiness of the world, the whole onflood or arrestment of humanity."

There was a pleasant-faced, fair-haired lady, of two or three and twenty, sitting upon the next seat across the aisle of the car. At this point she spoke up, addressing Mr. Sanders.

"Pardon," she said, "my mingling in your conversation; but I could not help but hear much of it yesterday, and I was greatly interested. I would like to ask you a question."

"Certainly," replied Mr. Sanders.

Mr. Hutchinson rose to his feet and said:

"Take my seat, madam, alongside of Mr. Sanders. You will hear better, and it does not affect me to ride backwards."

"Thank you," said the young lady, changing her place.

"I do not know," she continued, "anything about the financial questions, and I find many gentlemen equally ignorant; but I perceive that something is wrong. Three years ago my father was esteemed a rich man; now he is so poor that our family is broken up, and I am on my way to California to visit my father's brother, and hope to get a position as a teacher, so that I will not be a burden on any one. But I cannot understand why it is,

while the earth retains its fertility and mankind continue industrious, that labor cannot perpetually create wealth; why it is that food is less in price than the cost of producing it, and yet millions cannot secure enough to buy it?"

"I tried to show yesterday," replied Mr. Sanders, "that these evils are due to a limitation upon the governmental medium of exchange, called money; an artificial interference with the natural conditions you speak of; a something, created by man, which cries out to the earth, 'stop multiplying thy seed;' to the muscles of man, 'stop thy toil;' to the mine, 'close up thy mouth;' to the ship, 'sweep no more before the streaming and triumphant wind;' to the wild beasts, 'you are safe in your fastnesses, for man shall advance no more;' to the whole human family, 'stand still and shrink and suffer.' "

"But is there not," asked the young lady, "a deeper cause than all this? Why, at this stage of the world's development, should this great calamity burst forth upon the world?"

"You are right, madam," replied Mr. Sanders, "there is a deeper cause—a something grounded on the very nature of the animal man. It is

HUMAN SELFISHNESS.

"There are, we are told by the scientists, two great agencies operating upon the heavenly bodies—the centripetal force and centrifugal force; the one draws them together, and the other keeps them apart. The sun, by the first, would drag the earth into the fiery embrace of its gigantic flames; the other would send it flying off into boundless space. In the just balance and equipoise of these two huge powers the planets are held in their orbits and the harmony of the universe preserved.

"So there is in human nature a centripetal force of selfishness which draws everything to the individual, and a centrifugal force called philanthropy, which reaches out to the mass; and it is only by the interplay of these great powers that human society is possible.

"First, the brute animal, man, found the necessity of defending his own life against the whole world, in the prodigious and continuous battle of nature. Then the centrifugal force was enlarged to take in his wife and

children, and the smoke-blacked cave in the rock became
a home.   Then the family, in course of time, broadened
out into a clan, all kinsmen; thence into a tribe; thence
into a race; thence into a nation. These were all enlarge-
ments of the centripetal force. The people stood together
because they were of the same blood and spoke the same
tongue.   In some of the old countries to this day the
word 'friend' means a 'relative.' There could be no
fellowship that did not grow out of a kindred descent.
Then as civilization progressed the centrifugal force came
into play and the sense of what was best for the individual
or his brother expanded into what was best for all the
generations of men.   Man was forced out of himself into
consideration of the mass.   Then came Christianity
teaching the universal brotherhood of the occupants of
the earth, and that there was over all a common Father,
whose children, of all tongues and colors, were blood
kindred, clansmen, moulded of one substance after a common pattern.

"The curse of our age seems to be a rising up of the
centripetal force and a sweeping away of the centrifugal.
This is perhaps due to the very progress of civilization.
In the old time a man expected to die in the station in
which he was born; the peasant was always a peasant;
the prince forever a prince.   Now we have seen four poor
boys shake the bog mud from their unshod feet, cross the
ocean and the continent from Ireland to California, and
become rich beyond the dreams of emperors. We have
seen a Carrickfergus weaver, spare, half-fed, but full of
hereditary fire, migrate to America and fight a long hard
fight with fate for enough to eat, and die in the struggle;
but his son, who was wounded by an English officer
because he refused to clean his boots, became the hero of

New Orleans and President of the United States. And still later we saw a rail-splitter, dwelling in a hovel without doors, windows or floor, rise to be a 'true-born king of men;' a magnificent and tremendous genius. So that in this age all things are possible. The pauper becomes a prince and the prince a pauper. Life is an immense scramble, and the blowpipe of possibility blows the dull coals of intellect into the white flame of action. And all this tends to intensify the power which draws everything into the center of the individual, and the threads which tie man to his race and his age and his planet are melted in the fire of selfishness. Hence history becomes, in the main, a record of appalling brutalities, and the man who oppresses is respected and the man who is oppressed is despised. And science comes in, to gild with high-sounding phrases the rottenness of greed, 'and the survival of the fittest' is held a justification for the most ruthless barbarities; as if God himself had said, 'Kill them;' and Saturn, devouring his children, pushes the merciful Christ from his heavenly footstool.''

" That is strongly stated," said Mr. Hutchinson, "but is it true? Do the aristocracy deserve such a sweeping condemnation?"

" Deserve," replied the farmer, " why look at the case of Ireland! Look at the English landlord sitting with his legs around the huge pot-pie, indignantly glaring at the poor, humble peasant, because he has to give him a fragment to enable him to live. And yet the Irishman, by rights, owns the whole pie; his ancestors, for thousands of years, possessed the land from which the materials were raised that made the pie. It was wrested from him by superior weapons and greater numbers—confiscated. And on this confiscated land, as an humble tenant, he

has raised the mutton and the flour and potatoes that
made that pie. And see how the ogre indignantly regards him, because he insists on having something to eat
while he works! Why could not a slave be invented that
would toil without consuming? Steam and electricity
come pretty near it, but not quite. Oh, for a workman
all muscle and no stomach! Oh, for a cow all tenderloin
and milk-bag.

"Then look at London's swarming streets—the waxy-
faced, starving people—her own people—massed hungrily
on the corners or gathered around shop-windows—no two
of them allowed to stop and talk together on Trafalgar
square lest a mob assemble and the Empire disappear like
the dream of a dyspeptic! And yet England has her billions loaned abroad on which her tens of thousands live

in idle and magnificent luxury. One Englishman gluts and gorges and another Englishman starves and dies; and civilization and statesmanship propose no remedy And science prattles about the survival of the fittest, as if it was fore-ordained and inevitable.

"And *kraft*, power, degenerates into *craft*, cunning; and *king* is derived from the same root as *cunning*. No better man lives than the individual Englishman, but this ruling class, in all ages, has been cruel, arrogant and heartless; as merciless to its own people as it was to all the rest of the world. But we need not abuse them. They are worse than others probably because they have had more opportunity than others. The qualities that go to make oppression are simply inordinate selfishness,

which grabs all it sees and would make a dining table of the bodies of its dead victims. It has given up cannibalism, simply because there was an abundance of other kinds of food; but there isn't much difference between eating a man's body and devouring his substance so that he perishes. One is a physical, the other a moral cannibalism. And there are many men who would rather be eaten after death than eaten before death.

"But, oh! greed, greed, greed!

THE DARWINIAN THEORY.

"There has been a great deal of discussion of late

years as to the descent of man from the monkeys. The
monkey is a mean creature, we admit, a chattering, little,
inconsequential, dirty beast, but he does not begin to ex-
plain the human family. It would seem as if before man
was created, the elements that go to make up his character had already been developed and used in the animal
kingdom. Man was a special creation and no accident;
but just as his nerves, muscles and bones repeat, more or
less accurately, all the vertebrated creatures that had
lived on earth before him, so into his mental constitution
entered their various dispositions. And so in the genus
homo we will find the dash of the lion and the cowardice
of the jackal; the ferocity of the tiger and the gentleness
of the dove; the wisdom of the elephant and the fantastic
variety of the ape. Their very faces speak these various
lines of mental descent, and you will see lion-faced men
and horse-faced men and rabbit-faced men and giraffe-
headed men. You will also see ox-eyed women and
paroquet women, and 'the painted jays of Italy,' and
snake-eyed women and nightingale women. There is
nothing so like the female human, however, as the female
chicken. Their ways are a delicious caricature of the
creatures so dear to us. But if one were to ask me what
animal the successful plutocrat most closely resembled as
a class (of course there are exceptions) I should say—the
hog.''

"Oh, you certainly do not mean that," cried the young
lady.

"Only in a metaphorical sense, my dear madam," replied Mr. Sanders. "Paul tells us we have a temporal
body and a spiritual body. There are physical bristles
and moral bristles, and I have seen men—and some

women too—whose skins were smooth as paper and per-
fumed like the aroma

> 'Which told the world-seeking Genoese
> The Indian isles were nigh.'

And who yet, to the spiritual perception, were covered
with bristles and smelt of the sty. There is part of us
which even silks and satins will not cover. The greedy
men should go and look into a pig pen at feeding time;
and then, utterly abashed and ashamed, walk off and
kneel down and ask God to squeeze some of the dirt out of
his heart and give him less money and more soul, lest
when he reappears in this visible world it should be in a
sty.

"I remember a story of a farmer who took all the
prizes at the fairs around him for the great fatness of his
hogs. His emulous neighbors could not understand it;
they fed their swine all they would eat, but at a certain
point they stopped laying on fat. Nature had got all it
wanted and would go no farther. And so they proceeded to spy upon the successful pork-raiser to find his
secret. At length they discovered it; it was based on an
intimate acquaintance with hog and human intelligence.

"When his animals had reached the point attained by
his neighbors' swine, and lay down contentedly to enjoy
the sweets of 'tired nature's sweet restorer—balmy sleep
—the balm of hurt minds, great nature's second course,'
our ingenious friend put into the pen with him a poor,
half-starved, hungry shoat. Ah! Then all the instincts
of the millionaire were aroused in the porcine bosom.
What! That wretched razor-back wants to get fat too!
Call out the military! Where are Cleveland and Olney?
The very foundations of society are being subverted! All
hogs are *not* created equal; they are *not* entitled to the

equal pursuit of happiness; or if they are, they are not
entitled equally to catch up with it—they can pursue it as
much as they please.

"But, as the monster of flesh cannot telephone to the
administration at Washington, it does all that its environment will permit. It turns and gorges the food for which
before it had no appetite; it takes it in in great gobs; it
shovels it down its throat, presenting its unreasoning ex-

tremity to the poor razor-back from whatever quarter he
seeks to approach the trough.

"Oh, the human delight of monopolizing a superfluity
for which some one else is perishing! Think how exquisite it is! This it is that makes the Goulds and the
Vanderbilts and the Rockefellers spend nights and days
of ceaseless labor, while their brethren are squealing all
around them, and dying for a morsel of that of which
they have too much. And the society of the 400 is only a

kind of a hog-show, where men are rated by their financial weight, because it indicates how many shoats they have butted and bumped away from nature's universal trough, wherein enough was provided for all by the Great Farmer, who amuses Himself keeping hogs. It is most astonishing that God should make such creatures when there is no compulsion on him, and should put them into a world where there are saints and angels. It is a hing no man can understand.

THE HOG IN HUMAN NATURE.

"The hog in human nature is, indeed, 'the direful spring of woes unnumbered,' Eve ate the apple because she desired increase of knowledge. Adam ate it because he was hungry. God ought to have known the animal he had created too well to subject him to such a test. He might just as well damn us all to-day because a usurer took 100 per cent. per annum interest on a chattel mortgage. It was the hog in human nature that caused the Trojan war—that is, if it ever did occur—one hog running away with another hog's wife. It was the hog in human nature that sent the Roman eagles flying over the known world, turning warriors into peasants and peasants into slaves. It was the hog in human nature— and a bloody and brutal hog too—that set the gladiators loose to slaughter each other, and gave up Christian martyrs to the wild beasts. There is no record known, and no figures used by man that will tell, the incalculable miseries inflicted on mankind, through thousands of years, in all parts of the world, by the hnman hogs called kings and conquerors. They forced our forefathers to fly across the ocean, to the wilderness, to escape persecution for opinion's sake; and when, by their industry, the immigrants had transformed the wilderness into a garden, they followed them up to enslave them. But, glory be to God! the red-coated hogs went scudding back whence they came, with their pretty little tails in the air, redder than their coats with their own blood. And now, having found that cannon and guns cannot conquer us, they are ruining us by corrupting our Congress, and buying up our presidents, judges and newspapers. We need another 1776 revolution, and it is coming; and when the surrender at Yorktown is reached again, it will be a surrender of the monsters of the whole world, and a Declaration of Independence will be proclaimed for all mankind.

"Hogs! You can't go even into the day-car in front of us without seeing one or two of them. You will behold a great, fat fellow, with half a dozen bundles and valises. He has paid for one seat and he spreads himself over half a dozen. He puts his overcoat and umbrella in two seats across the aisle, and then he will tell the weary travelers who contemplate sitting down, that the two gentlemen who own the coat and umbrella have just stepped out, and will be back in a minute. He gets in early, unlocks one of the seats and turns it over, and spreads himself and bundles over four places, his noble endowment of feet distributed widely over two of them, while he pretends to go to sleep with his head next the window on a pile of valises, presenting the most difficult part of his person for an interview to those who have paid just as much for their passage as he has. And out of the corner of his eye he enjoys the sight of the crowd in the aisle—the pale woman with a child in her arms, the gray-haired old man, and all the rest; their misery is a kind of Worcestershire sauce to the palate of his enjoyment; he tastes it all the way down to his very boots.

Anarchy. Selfishness Rampant.

"But lo! Authority appears on the scene—the brake-man. He represents law, order, justice, fair play. He represents the community against the individual. He yanks the hog up by the neck, and seats him, growling and swearing, where his head was; he turns back the seat and piles coat, umbrella, bundles and valises all on top of their owner, until he sits imbedded in debris, scowling furiously at the poor weary people who were standing and have taken the seats they paid for.

"Selfishness has been suppressed. Anarchy is over-thrown. Law triumphs. Justice is made manifest.

"There is the solution of all our enigmas. We are all passengers together on this vehicle, the earth, which is rushing forward at the rate of one thousand miles an hour. We have all got our tickets from the President of the Company.

"The stamp of man on our faces is the imprint of equal-ity. No one passenger has any more rights than another. We are all God's poor children. Each is entitled to a place and a seat at the dining table. We have paid our way by being human. But the vehicle is all in confusion now. The hogs have seized ten times as much space and food as they are entitled to, and thousands are stand-ing and hungry. And the aggressors have hired a mul-titude of the idle and vicious to defend them with weapons, in their unjust possessions; and they have bribed the brakemen, and they do not see the protruding, offensive corporosity, or the poor, tired passengers, And the earth spins through space, while groans and cries and piteous appeals go up to God; and it is enfolded in misery as in a bloody garment; and it looks as if, in a little while, the hogs would be thrown out of the windows or the people be driven out onto the roof or the platforms.

" How beautiful it is to see a well-ordered railway car; every seat occupied by intelligent, courteous passengers; no crowding, no grumbling, no complaints, but civility and kindness everywhere. That is a picture of what this world can be made by the suppression of ' the hog in human nature.' But the law must step in and say to the brute, 'Thus far shalt thou go and no farther.' ' Here is room for all, and all must look after the equal rights of each.'

" This whole battle between gold and silver is nothing but the outcome of ' the hog in human nature.' "

" Indeed," said the young lady, " how do you prove that ? "

" Simply enough," replied Mr. Sanders.

THE GOLD AND SILVER QUESTION.

" Gold and silver were not made money by law. No international convention ever met, in the first instance, in the the past ages, and agreed to adopt them. As I said the other day, they were first the *sacred* metals of our ancestors, and then became the *precious* metals, because they were used to adorn the temples of the earth's greatest gods, the sun and the moon. Merchants bought them wherever they traded, along savage or civilized coasts, because they knew the priests, on their return home, would give them food and clothes and jewels for them. But their whole use is a survival of primeval superstition. Their beauty and compactness made them, it is true, desirable, and so they passed from hand to hand in a world-wide barter; and hence, when governments came to coin money, the stamp was naturally affixed to fragments of these convenient yellow and white metals. They were valuable before they were money, and money before they were coined;

and the barbarian races—rude and crude—had no idea
of money that could not be weighed and melted; like some
of our modern philosophers who will not believe there is
anything in the universe that is not a ponderable entity.
The limitations of their senses they mistake for the limitations of Divinity; and what they cannot see they swear is
not.   And hence we have a superstition of too little belief in place of the old-time superstition of too much belief.   One set of old women has been driven off, and
another set of old women, of the other sex, called philosophers, substituted in their place.

"Well," he continued, "just as the sun and moon moved
through the heavens, in silent and harmonious beauty—
the greater and the lesser lights—so these metals which
represented them, the one golden and sun-like, the other
silvern and moon-like, rode through the domain of human civilization, holding a relation in value much like
the relation of the sun and moon in apparent size and
power.   And as God permitted kings, as temporary leaders, until republics could be established, so he gave to
man the use of these metals, until the power and majesty
of vast and civilized peoples could be understood and
stamped upon paper, and the intrinsic money theory
forever relegated to the limbo of old world superstitions.

" But down the ages these two metals came hand in hand
for probably more than 20,000 years.   There is no doubt
they were the sacred metals of Atlantis eleven thousand
years ago; and the legends tell us that there were ten
thousand years between the settlement of Atlantis and its
destruction.   During many ages, when sun and moon
worship was the religion of all civilized peoples these metals
were honored next to the heavenly luminaries themselves.

" In all that vast lapse of time no attempt was ever

made to divorce them until a quarter of a century ago, except in one instance, and that was in the year 221 A. D., and the lessons it teaches are most prophetic. Through Egyptian, Assyrian, Grecian and Roman civilization, the yellow and the white metals moved hand in hand, as the basis of commerce and the symbols of wealth. But in A. D. 221, in the reign of a vile emperor, for the purpose of still farther oppressing the suffering tax-payers of Rome and its provinces, and increasing the value of the money in which the taxes were paid, it was resolved to demonetize silver and make gold the only legal tender. The consequences were very much the same as those which have overtaken ourselves. A recent writer says:

" ' Consequently prices fell lower and lower, the money-lenders received more and more in interest and principal, taxes became more and more burdensome, and producers were further discouraged by the constant depreciation of their property, which gradually fell into the hands of the creditor classes. The property of the producing classes being exhausted without paying their debts, they became the slaves of their creditors. All incentive to energy was destroyed and the classes that once formed the strength of Rome, from which the invincible legions were drawn —reduced as they were to slavery—were ready to welcome any change as a relief. At the same time while the producing classes were reduced to a state of slavery, the creditor classes fell into a state of growing moral corruption—a state that is always brought about by the possession of unearned gains. Thus reduced to impotency by slavery, ignorance, heathenism and moral corruption, the Roman Empire fell an easy victim to the hordes of barbaric Germans, who marched from one end of Italy to the other without meeting any serious resistance.'

THE ROMAN EMPIRE AND THE UNITED STATES COMPARED.

" Indeed if one desires to understand the dangers which

The Nemesis of Corruption.

threaten our present civilization he has but to peruse the pages of Roman history. In reading the following, from Froude's *Cæsar* (p. 6), we seem to have before us an almost exact picture of our own times:

" ' It was an age of material progress and material civilization; an age of civil liberty and intellectual culture; an age of pamphlets and epigrams, of salons and dinner parties, of senatorial majorities and electoral corruption. The highest offices of state were open, in theory, to the meanest citizen; they were confined, in fact, to those who had the longest purses, or the most ready use of the tongue on popular platforms. Distinctions of birth had been exchanged for *distinctions of wealth*. The struggles between plebians and patricians for equality of privilege were over, and a new division had been formed between the party of property and a party who desired a change in the structure of society. The free cultivators were disappearing from the soil. Italy was being absorbed *into vast estates*, held by a few favored families and cultivated by slaves, while the old agricultural population was driven off the land and was crowded into towns. The rich were extravagant, for life had ceased to have practical interest, except for its material pleasures; the occupation of the higher classes was to obtain money without labor and to spend it in idle enjoyment. Patriotism survived on the lips, but patriotism meant the ascendancy of the party which would maintain the existing order of things, or (the party which) would overthrow it for a more equal distribution of the good things which alone were valued. Religion, once the foundation of the laws and rule of personal conduct, had subsided into opinion. The educated in their hearts disbelieved it. Temples were still built with increasing splendor; the established forms were scrupulously observed. Public men spoke conventionally of Providence, that they might throw on their opponents the odium of impiety; but of genuine belief that life had any serious meaning, there was none remaining beyond the circle of the silent, patient, ignorant multitude. The whole spiritual atmosphere was saturated with cant—cant moral, cant political, cant religious; an affectation of high principle which had ceased to touch the conduct, and flowed on in an increasing volume of insincere and unreal speech. * * *

" 'The Romans ceased to believe, and in losing their faith they became as steel becomes when it is demagnetized, the spiritual quality was gone out of them, and the high society of Rome itself became a society of powerful animals with an enormous appetite for pleasure. Wealth poured in more and more, and luxury grew more unbounded. Palaces sprang up in the city, castles in the country, villas at pleasant places by the sea, and parks and fish ponds, and game preserves and gardens, and vast retinues of servants. When natural pleasures had been indulged in to satiety, pleasures which were against nature were imported from the East to stimulate the exhausted appetite. To make money—money by any means, lawful or unlawful—became the universal passion. * * *

" ' Moral habits are all-sufficient while they last; but with rude, strong natures they are but chains which hold the passions prisoners. Let the chain break, and the released brute is but the more powerful for evil from the force which his constitution has inherited. Money! The cry was still money! Money was the one thought from the highest senator to the poorest wretch who sold his vote in the Comitia. For money judges gave unjust decrees and juries gave corrupt verdicts. Governors held their provinces for one, two or three years; they went out bankrupt from extravagance, they returned with millions for fresh riot. To obtain a province was the first ambition of a Roman noble. The road to it lay through the prætorship and the consulship; these offices became, therefore, the prizes of the State, and being in the gift of the people they were sought after by means which demoralized alike the givers and the receivers. The elections were managed by clubs and coteries, and, except on occasions of national danger or political excitement those who spent most freely were most certain of success.'

"How precisely does all this depict the condition of affairs in the United States, in this year of grace 1895, over the whole land, from the Atlantic to the Pacific? One stumbling upon the passage, without the context, would swear that it referred to our own English-speaking people, instead of to a short, swarthy, sturdy, little race, living two thousand years ago on the Mediterranean, five thousand miles from our own shores.

"So precisely do events produce the same conditions that to read of the political struggles which followed in ancient Rome is to have presented to us a striking panorama of the great battle now being fought in this country.

Listen to this from the same author (Froude's ' *Cæsar*,' p. 20):

" ' Public spirit in the masses was dead or sleeping; the *commonwealth was a Plutocracy*. The free forms of *the* constitution were themselves the instruments of corrup-

tion. The rich were happy in the possession of all that
they could desire. The multitude was kept quiet by the
morsels of meat that were flung to it when it threatened
to be troublesome. The 'seven thousand in Israel,' the
few who in all states and all times remain pure in the
midst of evil, looked on with disgust, fearing that any
remedy which they might try might be worse than the
disease. * * * But it was not to be expected that
men of noble natures, young men especially, whose en-
thusiasm had not been controlled by experience, would sit
calmly by while their country was thus going headlong to
perdition. Redemption, if redemption was to be hoped
for, could only come from free citizens in the country dis-
tricts, whose manners and whose minds were still uncon-
taminated; in whom the ancient habits of life still survived; who still believed in the gods; who were content
to follow the wholesome round of honest labor. The
numbers of such citizens were fast dwindling away before
the omniverous appetite of the rich for territorial aggran-
disement. To rescue the land from the monopolists; to
renovate the old independent yeomanry; to prevent the
free population of Italy, out of which the legions had
been formed which had built up the empire, from being
pushed out of their places and supplanted by foreign
slaves, this, if it could be done, would restore the purity
of the constituency, snatch the elections from the control
of corruption, and rear up fresh generations of peasant
soldiers to preserve the liberties and the glories which
their fathers had won.' "

" Really," said the young lady, " that might be published as an essay, in one of our magazines, as a description of the present political conditions, with the change of
a word or two here and there."

" But," said Mr. Hutchinson, " the effort at reform
eventuated in Julius Cæsar and the Empire."

" That is true," replied Mr. Sanders, " but the root of
the evil was the corruption of the aristocracy, which, in
turn, degraded and demoralized the common people, and

ended in universal rottenness. This destroyed the republic, and it finally overthrew the empire, and brought in the barbarians and chaos and old night. It was brutal selfishness, 'the hog in human nature,' which blindly rooted out the foundations of the temple of civilization and brought it down in ruin on its own head.

THE SUN AND MOON.

"But the point I was trying to call your attention to was that, just as the sun and moon moved together through the heavens, so these, their typical metals, moved side by side, for hundreds of centuries, in the affairs of mankind; and that it would be as great an invasion of the orderly arrangements of nature to seek to pluck the moon from its orbit as it was to tear the white metal from the commercial firmament.

"If any great cause had rendered it probable that such a course would be advantageous to mankind, then it would have been proper for the civilized nations to have fully considered it, in newspapers, conventions, legislative chambers, and in discussions by a million firesides; weighing carefully all the arguments for and against such a step, before taking action upon it. See the tremendous debate that is now going on, all over the world, as to the restoration of silver to its ancient orbit. Even such a debate, with such a clamor of tongues, with such an array of facts, figures and authorities, should have preceded any attempt to tear it out of the commercial sky. Instead of that, silver was not the victim of an open and public war; it was secretly slain by the stilettos of hired banditti, in the darkness of the night."

HOW SILVER WAS DEMONETIZED.

"That charge," said Mr. Hutchinson, "has been made a hundred times and a hundred times disproved."

"Yes," said the young lady, "I read an article on the subject in 'The Light of Zion,' the day before I left home, which clearly shows that it was publicly repealed with the full knowledge of the whole country. I do not know much upon the subject myself, but I cannot believe a respectable newspaper would misrepresent the facts."

"Misrepresent!" cried Mr. Sanders; "why, my dear young lady, the newspapers of to-day would misrepresent anything. If there was any considerable sum of money to be made by it they would unite in denying the existence of God! If a million dollars were at stake they would so blackguard the memory of George Washington that the State of Virginia would rise up and throw his ashes into the Potomac! 'Misrepresent!' God gave man the alphabet, and the devil gave him the daily press. The first widens the area of his knowledge and the second perverts truth and darkens understanding.

"But here," he continued, "is the proof that the demonetization of silver was a secret fraud and trick and crime. Go search all the newspapers of the United States for the year 1873, for weeks and months before and after the passage of the act, and you cannot find the slightest reference to the fact that the mints of the United States had been closed against the coinage of a money-metal more ancient than the pyramids or the tower of Babel. Not a word; not a syllable. There were numerous telegrams from Washington, at that time, on all sorts of inconsequential matters, but not a sentence as to a change in our laws which is now widely and deeply agitating the people of our whole country, and indirectly of the whole world.

"Take all the platforms, state or national, of all the parties, since the formation of our government down to

and including 1873, and I challenge the defenders of this iniquity to put their fingers upon a single declaration demanding the demonetization of silver, or demanding anything hostile to the white metal. There is nothing of the kind. By what right did Congress dare to make such a radical and fundamental change in the financial system of this country without being urged to do so by any political party of any kind? Nothing but bribery and corruption of the rankest description could account for such a step.

" Call the roll of all the eminent men of this nation, since the constitution was adopted, down to and including 1873—men of all creeds and parties and sections— and where can a word or a line be quoted from any of their written or spoken utterances, asking that the doors of the mints be closed in the face of the prehistoric white metal? There is not one. Do you know of any ? "

" I cannot say I do," replied Mr. Hutchinson.

" Well, do you know of any declaration of any platform, prior to 1873, demanding the demonetization of silver ? "

" I have not looked into the matter," said Mr. Hutchinson, " and therefore cannot answer your question."

" I will go a step farther," said Mr. Sanders. " I undertake to say that from 1873 to this hour no national political party has ever dared to commend or make itself responsible for that act of 1873, or to sustain the demonetization of silver, except by trick and indirection."

" Do you mean to say," inquired the banker, " that the Republican party did not, in 1892, declare for the gold standard ? "

"Certainly not," said the farmer. "Here is what they said (consulting his note book):

"'The American people, from tradition and interest, favor bi-metallism, and the Republican party demands the use of both gold and silver as standard money, with restrictions and under such provisions to be determined by legislation, as will secure the maintenance of the parity of values of the two metals, so that the purchasing and debt-paying power of the dollar, whether of silver, gold or paper, shall be at all times equal.'"

"Ah," said Mr. Hutchinson, "there you see the proviso is bigger than the resolution."

"I have no doubt," was the reply, "that the man who drew that plank intended it for a trick and a subterfuge; but even then there is no approval of the act of 1873, and there is nothing in it inconsistent with the restoration of silver to its ancient position."

"I do not so understand it," said the other. "Observe what it says about 'parity of values' and debt-paying powers. Does not that mean demonetization of silver?"

"I do not undertake to say," was the reply, "what the trickster meant who drew it, but the resolution, I repeat, is not inconsistent with true bi-metallism. The 'parity of values' we had at all times prior to 1873. If there was any difference it was on the side of silver, which was at a premium over gold when it was demonetized. And even now, in spite of demonetization, the silver dollar in this country is at a parity of value with the gold dollar, and yet there is no law to compel the government to redeem silver in gold."

"Do you mean to say," inquired the young lady traveler, "that silver was worth more than gold when it was denied the right of being coined?"

"Certainly," said Mr. Sanders. "That is well understood."

"What excuse was there, then," she inquired, "for demonetizing silver, especially if no political party and no leading statesmen had demanded it?"

"There was none. It was sheer villainy. Not even the supple newspapers asked for anything of the kind. In the midst of silence, and in the darkness of the night, the evil deed was consummated, and to this hour nobody will stand sponsor for it."

"I deny," said Mr. Hutchinson, "that it was done in the darkness of the night."

TESTIMONY OF OUR LEADING STATESMEN.

"Well," replied the farmer, "I have here (consulting his note book) the testimony of the leading members of the House and Senate at that time, of both parties. I will first summon a leading Republican, Judge Kelly, of Philadelphia, the great protectionist; 'Pig-iron Kelly' he was called, a very able and honest man. I find by the Congressional Record, volume 7, part 2, 45th Congress, second session, page 1605, that he said:

"In connection with the charge that I advocated the bill which demonetized the standard silver dollar, I say that, though the chairman of the Committee on Coinage, I was as ignorant of the fact that it would demonetize the silver dollar or of its dropping the silver dollar from our system of coins as were those distinguished Senators, Messrs. Blaine and Voorhees, who were then members of the House, and each of whom, a few days since, interrogated the other: 'Did you know it was dropped when the bill passed?' 'No,' said Mr. Blaine. 'Did you?' 'No,' said Mr. Voorhees, 'I do not think there were three members in the house that knew it. I doubt whether Mr. Hooper, who, in my absence from the Committee on Coinage and attendance on the Committee on Ways and Means, managed the bill, knew it.   I say this in justice to him."

In the Congressional Record, February 15, 1878, page 1063, may be found the following:—

Mr. Voorhees.   I want to ask my friend from Maine, whom I am glad to designate that way, whether I may call him as one more witness to the fact that it was not generally known whether silver was demonetized.   Did he know, as the Speaker of the House, presiding at that time, that the silver dollar was demonetized in the bill to which he alludes?"

"Mr. Blaine.   'I did not know anything that was in the bill at all.   As I have said before, little was known or cared on the subject.   [Laughter.]   And now I should like to exchange questions with the Senator from Indiana, who was then on the floor and whose business, far more than mine, it was to know, because by the designation of the house I was to put the question; the Senator from Indiana, then on the floor of the House, with his power as a debater, was to unfold them to the House,   Did he know?'

"Mr. Voorhees.   I frankly say that I did not."

"But I see," replied Mr. Hutchinson, "that Prof. Laughlin quotes from another speech, made by Mr. Blaine, to the effect that the bill was discussed and its purpose understood.'

"Yes," replied Mr. Sanders, "Mr. Blaine, as a public man, was bound to defend his party from the charge of having consummated such an iniquity; but he does not deny that he said just what is set down in the Congressional Record, p. 1063, February 15, 1878, that he 'did not know anything that was in the bill at all—little was known or cared on the subject.'   Think of the Speaker of the House, the leader of his party, subsequently its candidate for the presidency, putting the question on the

passage of the bill, and not knowing that it closed the
mints of the United States against a metal which had been
the money of all civilized nations, at a time when his
ancestors were naked barbarians, possibly cannibals ! And
if he did not know anything that was in the bill, how
could less prominent and less able men, in Congress, be
expected to know anything about it ? And how much
more improbable was it that the great mass of the American people, hundreds and thousands of miles distant from
Washington, knew what was going on.

" But I continue the testimony:

" Senator Beck of Kentucky, Congressional Record, volume 7, part 1, Forty-fifth Congress, second session, page
260, said:

" It [the bill demonetizing silver] never was understood
by either House of Congress.   I say that with full knowledge of the facts.   No newspaper reporter—and they are
the most vigilant men I ever saw in obtaining information—discovered that it had been done."

" Mr. Burchard of Illinois, Congressional Record, July
13, 1876, volume 4, part 5, page 4560, said:—

" The Coinage act of 1873, unaccompanied by any written report upon the subject from any committee, and unknown to the members of Congress who, without opposition, allowed it to pass under the belief, if not assurance,
that it made no alteration in the value of the current
coins, changed the unit of value from silver to gold."

"Mr. Holmes of Indiana, Congressional Record, volume
4, part 6, Forty-fourth Congress, first session, Appendix,
page 193, said:—

" I have before me the record of the proceedings of this
House of the passage of that measure, which no man can
read without being convinced that the measure and the
method of its passage through this House was a ' colossal
swindle.'   I assert that the measure never had the sanc-

tion of this House, and it does not possess the moral force of law.''

"Joseph Cannon, Congressional Record, volume 4, part 6, Forty-fourth Congress, first session, Appendix, page 197, said:

"This legislation was had in the Forty-second Congress, February 12, 1873, by a bill to regulate the mints of the United States, and practically abolished silver as money by failing to provide for the coinage of the silver dollar. It was not discussed, as shown by the Record, and neither members of Congress nor the people understood the scope of the legislation.''

"Senator Voorhees of Indiana, Congressional Record, January 15, 1878, page 332, said:—

"The silver dollar is peculiarly the laboring man's dollar, as far as he may desire specie.   *   *   *
Throughout all the financial panics that have assailed this country, no man has been bold enough to raise his hand to strike it down; no man has ever dared to whisper of a contemplated assault upon it; and when the 12th day of February, 1873, approached, the day of doom to the American dollar, the dollar of our fathers, how silent was the work of the enemy! Not a sound, not a word, no note of warning to the American people that their favorite coin was about to be destroyed as money; that the greatest financial revolution of modern times was in contemplation and about to be accomplished against their highest and dearest rights! The tax payers of the United States were no more notified or consulted on this momentous measure than the slaves on a southern plantation before the war, when their master made up his mind to increase their task or to change them from a corn to a cotton field.

"Never since the foundation of the Government has a law of such vital and tremendous import, or indeed of any importance at all, crawled into our statute books so furtively and noiselessly as this. Its enactment there was as completely unknown to the people, and indeed to four-fifths of Congress itself, as the presence of a burglar in a house at midnight to its sleeping inmates. This was rendered possible partly because the clandestine movement was so utterly unexpected, and partly from the nature of the bill in which it occurred. The silver dollar of American history was demonetized in an act entitled ' An act revising and amending the laws relative to the mints, assay-offices, and coinage of the United States.'

"Senator Beck, of Kentucky, Congressional Record January 11, 1879, page 258, said:

" ' I know that the bondholders and monopolists of the country are seeking to destroy all the industries of the people in their greed to enhance the value of their gold. I know that the act of 1873 did more than all else to accomplish that result, and the demonetization act of the Revised Statutes was an illegal and unconstitutional consummation of the fraud. I want to restore that money to where it was before, and thus aid in preventing the consummation of their designs.'

"Senator Allison, of Iowa, Congressional Record, volume 7, part 2, Forty-fifth Congress, 2d session, page 1085, said:

" ' But when the secret history of this act of 1873 comes to be told, it will disclose the fact that the House of Representatives intended to coin both gold and silver, and intended to place both metals upon the French relation instead of our own, which was the true scientific position with reference to this subject in 1873, but that the bill was doctored, if I may use the term, and I use it in no offensive sense, of course.

*   *   *   *   *   *

" ' I said I used the word in no offensive sense. It was changed after the discussion, and the dollar of 420 grains was substituted for it.'

" Mr. Bright, of Tennessee, Congressional Record, volume 7, part 1, 2d session, Forty-fifth Congress, page 584, said:

"'It passed by fraud in the House, never having been printed in advance, being a substitute for the printed bill; never having been read at the clerk's desk, the reading having been dispensed with by an impression that the bill was no material alteration in the coinage laws; it was passed without discussion, debate being cut off by operation of the previous question. It was passed, to my certain information, under such circumstances that the fraud escaped the attention of some of the most watchful as well as the ablest statesmen in Congress at the time. * * * Aye, sir, it was a fraud that smells to heaven. It was a fraud that will stink in the nose of posterity, and for which some persons must give an account in the day of retribution.'"

HOW THE CRIME WAS ACCOMPLISHED.

"That the demonetization of silver was, as these Congressional witnesses testify (and every word, be it observed, is taken from the official record, page and book given), that it was, I say, a 'colossal swindle,' the work of a 'burglar in the house at midnight,' is shown by the very nature of the bill. Was it entitled 'an act to demonetize silver?' Not at all. It seemed to be purely a measure in relation to the mints and the details of coinage. Nor does it anywhere appear that the act, by any section or part of section, pronounces the doom of the white metal in any direct fashion. Not at all. The deadly work is accomplished not by a declaration of purpose or principle, but by *an omission*, in a catalogue of coins, to name the standard silver dollar of the fathers! Here is the cunning shape in which the villainy hides itself—this is the language that did the work we are all lamenting to-day:

"'That the gold coins of the United States shall be a one dollar piece, which, at the weight of twenty-five and eight-tenth grains shall be the unit of value.

" 'That the silver coins of the United States shall be a trade dollar, a half dollar or fifty-cent piece, a quarter dollar or twenty-five-cent piece, a dime or ten-cent piece; and said coins shall be a legal tender at their nominal value for any amount *not exceeding five dollars* in any one payment.

" 'That no coins, either of gold or silver, or minor coinage shall hereafter be issued from the mint, other than those of the denominations, standards and weights herein set forth.' (17 statutes, 424).

" Imagine an honest member of Congress trying, in the midst of the uproar of legislation, to keep track of what that bill meant. He could only do so by comparing it word for word with the existing statute; thereby he might have discovered that the standard dollar was omitted from the list of silver coins.

PRESIDENT GRANT'S TESTIMONY.

" Even the President of the United States, the magnanimous hero of the civil war, Ulysses S. Grant, who signed the demonetization act of 1873—and without whose signature it could not have become a law—did not know that it had demonetized silver; and eight months after he had signed the fatal act, on October 6, 1873, he wrote a letter to Mr. Cowdrey, in which he shows that he thought the poor, disqualified, proscribed white metal was still ' a standard of value the world over.' Here is his letter:

" 'I wonder that silver is not already coming into the market to supply the deficiency in the circulating medium. * * * Experience has proved that it takes about $40,000,000 of fractional currency to make the small change necessary for the transaction of the business of the country. Silver will gradually take the place of this currency, and, further, will become the standard of values, which will be hoarded in a small way. I estimate that

this will consume from $200,000,000 to $300,000,000 in
time of this species of our circulating medium. * * I
confess a desire to see a limited hoarding of money. But
I want to see a hoarding of something that is a standard
of value the world over.   Silver is this.

"'Our mines are now producing almost unlimited
amounts of silver, and it is becoming a question, 'What
shall we do with it?' I here suggest a solution which
will answer for some years to put it in circulation, keeping it there until it is fixed, and then we will find other
markets.' (See page 208, Congressional Record, December 14, 1877).

"But our Republican newspapers," said Mr. Hutchinson, "have claimed that whole columns of the Congressional Record were devoted to the discussion of the
bill."

"That is another trick," replied the farmer; "a bill to
codify existing laws as to the mints had been up before
two or three successive congresses, and had been discussed,
but the discussion did not touch the question of the demonetization of silver. Indeed, the bill of 1873 as it
passed the house contained the standard silver dollar, but,
as Senator Allison says, it was '*doctored*' in the Senate,
and the standard dollar was stricken out and the 'trade
dollar' substituted, and this was declared legal tender
only for debts of five dollars or less. There is where the
knife went in."

THE TRADE DOLLAR.

"What was the trade dollar?" inquired the young
lady.

"It was called the 'trick dollar,'" replied Mr. Sanders. "It contained 420 grains of silver, while the standard dollar contained only 412½ grains. It was part of
the work of the conspiracy. It was coined on the pre-

tense that it would be preferred by the people of China and India, in trade, because it contained more silver, It was really made to fit into the niche of the demonetization of the standard dollar. It was easier to slip in 'trade' for 'standard' in the act than to name no silver dollar of any kind. That vacuum might attract attention.''

''What became of the trade dollar?'' inquired the young lady. '' I do not remember seeing any of them.''

''No; they soon disappeared,'' replied Mr. Sanders. ''Three years after they had been fraudulently used to displace our legal tender dollars, the subservient Congress passed an act, July, 1876, which provided that ' the trade dollar shall not hereafter be a legal tender.' That finished their hash.''

''How so?'' said the young lady.

''The bankers, Mr. Hutchinson's brethren,'' said Mr. Sanders with a smile, ''having deprived them of their legal tender character, and the object for which they had been coined having been accomplished, refused to take them for more than 90 cents on the dollar; and the price at once fell to that. They showed great magnanimity; they might just as well have made it 40 cents on the dollar. Every one who had a legal tender dollar had to take it to a bank and swap it for ninety cents, and take his pay in standard dollars. Thus he exchanged 420 grains of silver for 412½ at a discount of 10 per cent.; gave more for less and paid a bonus to effect the trade.''

''Why,'' said the young lady, '' I thought the value of money was fixed by the intrinsic value of the metals of which it was composed.''

''All nonsense,'' replied the farmer. '' There is the

demonstration of it.   The coin with $7\frac{1}{2}$ grains more of
silver in it would not circulate at all, because it was not
legal tender, while the coin with the $7\frac{1}{2}$ grains less silver, being legal tender, is worth 10 per cent. more than
the coin of greater intrinsic value.   Intrinsic humbug !"

"Ah, there is the mistake all your school of statesmen
make," said Mr. Hutchinson.   "You rest all your faith
on 'fiat.'   But it is time to give up the discussion.   I see
our young friend is yawning.   Let us resume the subject
to-morrow."

"I am not at all tired," replied the young lady.   "Indeed, I am intensely interested.   I have obtained many
new ideas.   We women are going to vote some day, and
we should inform ourselves on all governmental questions."

THE FOURTH DAY.

"FIAT."

The debate of the two previous days had attracted a
good deal of attention from the other passengers on the
car, on whose hands time hung heavily; and, after breakfast, they gathered as near as they could to section 7, sitting in the vacant seats or standing up and listening.   The
young lady, whose name it seems was Miss Bowman, resumed her usual place.

"Well," said Mr. Hutchinson, "are you ready to go
on with the discussion?"

"Certainly," replied Mr. Sanders.   "Let me see.   What
were we to talk about this morning?"

"I think," said Miss Bowman, "it was about fiat-
money."

"Yes," said a sharp-nosed gentleman, "I would like to

hear that p'int debated. I don't believe in no fiat. We must have intrinsic money.''

"What is your business," inquired Mr. Sanders.

"Well, I have no partic'lar business. I have some money loaned out in Californy. It keeps me busy a lookin' after it.''

"I thought so," replied the farmer; "now do you know what 'fiat' is?''

"Yes," replied the other, "it is paper money, continental currency, assignats.''

"Not at all," said Mr. Sanders; "'fiat' means a command—a decree. The greatest fiatist we have any record of is the Almighty, for he made the universe out of nothing by his mere word. If some of our gold-bug statesmen had been present when he said 'Let there be light' they would have interrupted the proceedings, risen to a point of order and remarked that the Lord could not make light by a 'fiat'—there had got to be 'intrinsic value' somewhere. Now, what God is to Nature, so, on a smaller scale, is the congregated will of a people, called the government, to all the people of that country. It cannot, like God, make something out of nothing, but it can make a great deal out of very little; it can give to a piece of paper so much value that men will readily exchange for it gold and silver and diamonds and pearls and land and houses and all things that are regarded as valuables on earth.''

"You mean paper money?" asked Mr. Hutchinson.

"No," was the reply; "I have not come to that yet—I mean government bonds.''

"Ah," said the banker, "they are valuable because they contain a contract that they are to be paid in gold.''

"There is no United States bond," said Mr. Sanders, "that contains a contract that it is payable in gold. They are all payable in *coin*, and silver is coin as much as gold."

"But then both the Republican and Democratic administrations," said Mr. Hutchinson, "have interpreted that to mean gold."

"I know they have; and they have done it in obedience to the money-power, without authority from law, and to the great detriment of the people of this country. But that is only an unworthy trick, and rests simply upon the patient acquiescence of the tax-payers, and no one can tell how long that will last. And it must be remembered that the further off the payment of the bond, in coin, is postponed, by the terms thereof, the more valuable is the bond. A twenty-year bond is worth more than one for ten years, and one for a hundred years at one per cent. would command a large premium over any existing issues. It is, therefore, evident that the capitalist noes not want the coin but the bond. But I have proved my proposition, that the ' fiat ' of government impressed on a piece of paper, worth one mill, or the tenth of a cent, can make it worth one hundred thousand dollars. And the ' fiat ' of government can take you, sir," continued Mr. Sanders, turning fiercely to the peak-nosed man, "and set you, like Uriah, in the fore-front of battle, to be shot down like a dog."

"How can they do that?"

"Just as they did with hundreds of thousands during the civil war—they would draft you."

"Ah!" said peak-nose, "that is a military necessity."

"Well," said Mr. Sanders, "is not the life of the nation a military necessity, whether assailed by the cannon of open and foreign enemies, or the trickeries and knaveries of domestic and secret foes? The coat of formal expression of the popular will, which we call constitution and law, has no right to prove a shirt of Nessus and kill the Hercules (the people) for whose protection it was intended. But everything rests on the *fiat* of government. It is the biggest thing, next to God, on the planet. The very sneerers at popular rights exist by means of it."

" How so?" said the peak-nosed man.

" Because your life and mine would not be worth an hour's purchase if the fiat of the government did not decree that we should be protected. It is the fiat, the command, the authority of the consolidated people, that represses the robbers and murderers. Repeal all law, and we would be mobbed at the next station this train stops at, and despoiled of our possessions and probably slain. The same greed that inspires the money-lender would inspire the non-capitalistic class to plunder the money lender. They would foreclose on him with a revolver or enjoin him with a bowie knife; and he could take his writ of certiorari to the Almighty and try it during eternity. Fiat," continued Mr. Sanders, " why, the government can take you, on the charge of violating the laws of the land, and whether guilty or not, hang you up by the neck before an admiring audience, until you are choked to death.

"Fiat! Fiat!" he continued. " Why, all that you are, all that you have, all that you will be in this world; the safety of wife, children, property, peace, order, culture, civilization; the very bread you eat and the boots on your feet represent fiat; and it makes me mad all over to hear nincompoops sneering at fiat, and declaring that this government of 70,000,000 people, with power to issue legal tender money, good for all debts public and private, cannot create money unless it promises to redeem it in a yellow accident called gold. Redeemed! Why a greenback is redeemed every time the government receives it for taxes; every time A pays a debt to B with it; every time it is exchanged for wheat and pork and flour and woolen and cotton goods, or all these hundreds of things that constitute the real wealth of the country, of which money is but the conventional shadow, type and figure."

"You surprise me," said Miss Bowman. "I thought gold was the real wealth."

"Yes," said Mr. Sanders, "that is the poisonous nonsense which is poured into the porches of the ears of the sleeping Hamlet—the people. But test it. Take one of these wordiferous editors, filling all space with resounding lies, at $25 a week, and put him down on a desert island, with $100,000 in gold pieces and nothing else. Let him starve for three or four days, and he would give his whole pile for a square meal of potatoes and corn bread; and finally realize, in his death agonies, that wealth consists of those things which are necessary for man's life, and that gold is a mere conventional symbol, with no value save what the common consent of society gives it. When Columbus landed on one of the West Indian islands a sailor exchanged an iron nail for a big piece of gold, and the savage, as soon as the trade was completed, ran away like a deer, to escape, before the sailor had discovered how worthless was the stuff he had given him, in comparison with a piece of that wonderful metal, iron.

"No," continued Mr. Sanders; "the farmer who makes twenty bushels of wheat (food) grow where one is sown;

and the mechanic who turns wool and cotton and flax into cloth to protect the human frame from heat or cold; or the workman who converts the growing forest trees into houses, or the ore of the mine into implements or machinery—these add to the *wealth* of the world, for they produce those things without which civilization could not endure. But the man who brings money into the country simply makes slaves.''

BORROWED MONEY BREEDS SLAVES.

"Makes slaves!" cried Mr. Hutchinson.

"Yes," replied the farmer, "for he will not put it out until human beings agree to work for it; and the man who works for another, without compensation, is a slave, whether you can sell him on the auction block or not.''

"Such utterances astonish me," said Mr. Hutchinson. "Look at the money invested in railroad building in this country. The nation could not have been developed without it. Does that make slaves?''

"Certainly," was the reply. "The railroad bonds are simply a blanket mortgage put upon the immense areas of country through which the road passes; and the people living thereon have to work from early youth to the grave to pay the interest on the same; aud when they die they transmit the burden to the shoulders of their children, and they in turn to theirs. And they not only have to pay interest on the money actually invested in the construction of the road, but on as much more, or twice as much more, of 'watered stock,' for which not one dollar was ever paid. They are thus doubly slaves—slaves to a real debt and slaves to a bogus debt; slaves to fact and slaves to fiction; slaves to substance and slaves to shadow.''

" But how do you make out," said the peak-nosed man, "that the people pay any such interest?"

" Easily enough," replied Mr. Sanders. " In our vast inter-continental regions—and that term applies to four-fifths of this great country—those who dwell in a territory traversed by a railroad cannot communicate with the external world except by that means of transportation. Every time they leave their habitat they pay tribute to the corporation. Everything they sell, that goes outside their immediate neighborhood, has to go over that road; and everything they buy has to come over it; and as the charges on all this transportation have to be great enough to pay the expenses of running the road and repairing it, and the interest on the real debt and the interest on the bogus debt, it all comes out of the tributary population, who are life-long slaves of invested capital, and its shadow, unreal capital."

" Must we not have railroads?" asked Mr. Hutchinson.

" Yes; but if the egregious vanity of our people, and their belief that numbers was synonymous with greatness, had not misled them, the co-operation of industry and natural resources: the plowman and the soil; the mine and the miner; the mechanic and his materials, would have developed tremendous wealth, and the people could have built their own railroads as rapidly as the real development of the country demanded, instead of becoming the bondsmen of foreigners. See the unparalleled growth of our country during the first half of this century. See the States that were cleared of forests, the homes that sprang up, all over New York, Pennsylvania, Ohio, Indiana, Michigan, Virginia and the southern States; the great public highways built by the national government, or the canals dug by the State governments. Remember the vast crops of wheat and cotton and meats that were shipped abroad, bringing in immense quantities of gold and silver from the old world. How changed now, when our entire crops, at their market price, will not pay the interest on our foreign indebtedness; when millions of our people are tramps; when British capital owns our mills, our mines, our railroads, our breweries, and, (happy combination!) even our newspapers; when Uncle Sam stands trembling before the Rothschilds, to know whether or not they will save the great republic of the world from bankruptcy; and when, in the near future, we can behold a vision of free institutions kicked off the face of the planet by John Bull and the Money-Lenders.

"God give us back the simplicity, the purity and the prosperity of the early days, when Jefferson rode to the Capitol to be inaugurated (after blacking his own boots) on horseback; when Andrew Jackson hurled the conquerors of Napoleon pell mell out of the valley of the Mississippi, and then proceeded to crush the head of the giant serpent of Plutocracy, represented by the National Bank and smashed the reign of corruption for a generation. Would that we could call up old Andy from his grave."

"'One blast upon his bugle horn
Were worth a million men.'"

"But, my dear sir," said Mr. Hutchinson, "you are wandering from the subject—that was, the power of the government to create money by its fiat, apart from intrinsic value."

"Intrinsic value," was the reply. "What intrinsic value is there in gold and silver?"

"Complete and absolute," said Mr. Hutchinson.

THE INTRINSIC VALUE OF GOLD AND SILVER.

"I deny it," replied Mr. Sanders. "The value of the

WHAT WE ARE COMING TO.

John Bull: Get off the planet, you bold fraud. You were conceived in a blunder and your existence is a reproach to the money-power of the world. Get bout!

Rothschilds: Gei away wit you! Der is no God but Mammon, and John and me are his prophets. Here, take your " Teclaration of Independence mit you. All a lot of lies.

so-called precious metals is simply that given them by the consensus of the opinions of mankind.''

"What is your proof of that?" asked the peak-nosed man.

" The history of silver,'' replied Mr. Sa. lers. " So long as it had equal access to the mints with gold it kept side by side with gold, in value, at the proportion fixed by the nations. The moment the mints of a large part of the world were shut against silver it began to fall and fell to one-half its previous price. If its use as money in Europe, Asia, Africa, America and Oceanica was totally discontinued it would not be worth as much as tin. For of what use is it?''

" It would be used for ornaments,'' said the young lady.

" Do you wear decorations of tin or lead or copper or brass?'' replied the farmer.

" No—they are too cheap.''

"Precisely,'' said Mr. Sanders, " and if there was no market or use for silver any more than there is for tin or lead or brass, and it was equally cheap, it would be a disgrace to ornament one's self with it. If the demonetization of gold had continued——''

" What are you talking about?'' said the peak-nosed man.

" I mean just what I say,'' retorted the farmer, " gold was once demonetized over a large part of Europe, and if that demonetization had gone as far as the demonetization of silver has to-day, it would have fallen off one-half or more in price, just as silver has.''

"The demonetization of gold! I never heard of that.'' said Miss Bowman.

" Nor I,'' said the peak-nosed man.

GOLD DEMONETIZED.

" The discovery of gold in California and Australia,''

replied Mr. Sanders, "in 1849 and 1850, resulted in the pouring fourth of unlimited quantities of that money, which largely found their way to Europe. The bankers took alarm. It seemed as if the heavens had broken open and were raining gold. The shrewd leaders of the financiers said; 'This will not do. Abundant money means cheap money. When money is cheap it will buy less of the products of human industry; prices rise; the people get out of debt; our money is thrown back on our hands and we cannot rent it out for large interest; it is useless to us; we cannot live on our accumulations; we will have to go to work on equal terms with the rest of mankind. We must, therefore, demonetize this over plentiful metal, gold, and make silver, the scarcer element, the basis of the world's business.' Prof. Levi says:

"'Frightened, and not without reason, at the possible consequences, some countries heretofore anxious to attract and retain gold in circulation, even at great sacrifice, showed a feverish anxiety to banish it altogether. In July, 1850, Holland demonetized the ten-florin piece and the Guillame; Portugal prohibited any gold from having current value except the English sovereign; Belgium demonetized her gold circulation (that is, repealed the laws making it legal money); Russia prohibited the export of silver; and France, alarmed but less hasty, issued a commission to look into the matter.'

'In 1855 Germany demonetized gold and made silver the only legal money. Even in England numerous cabinet meetings were held to consider the advisability of doing the same thing. But it was soon learned that the gold supplies were principally surface deposits, and the yellow flood began to decrease; and the nations of Europe took the back track. Then came the large production of silver in Nevada, and the bankers said: 'Gold is to be the scarce metal and silver the abundant one; therefore we must remonetize gold and demonetize silver.' ''

"I am very much surprised, said Miss Bowman. "I have read so much in the daily press in praise of gold and in denunciation of silver, that I can scarcely think it possible that only forty-five or fifty years ago the very men who are now trying to crucify silver, and drive it out of existence, were ready to make it the sole money metal of the world, and reduce gold to the position of a proscribed commodity. Are you sure of your facts?"

"Perfectly sure. I will ask Mr. Hutchinson whether the statements I have made as to the demonetization of gold in 1850–1855 are not true."

"I believe they are," replied Mr. Hutchinson.

"And the motives were as I have given them?"

"Well, I do not care to go into those questions," replied the banker.

"You will at least admit," said Mr. Sanders, "that the warfare upon gold at that time was because it was supposed it would be the more abundant metal."

"I suppose that can hardly be disputed," replied Mr. Hutchinson.

"Now," said the farmer, turning to the peak-nosed man, "suppose this recent story now going the rounds of the press, proved true,—that the whole American beach of the Pacific ocean, for 5,000 miles, is largely made up of gold washings, and that gold was about to become as abundant and as cheap as copper, do you think you would still advocate gold-monometalism?"

"Not at all," was the reply. "I would go in for silver-monometalism."

"But suppose mountains of solid silver were discovered in Alaska, what then?"

"Then I should be in favor of a limited issue of green-backs."

"Then," said the farmer, "your whole policy would be to make money out of something that could not be abundant."

"Exactly," said the other, "how could I lend my money out and live on the interest of it if every man was prosperous and had his pockets full of cash. I must look out for my own interests."

"And must not the people look out for their interests?"

"Certainly."

"And their interest is diametrically opposite to yours."

"How do you make that out?"

"You want scarce money; they want abundant money. They want everybody out of debt; you want all those who have any assets in a condition that they will be forced to borrow from you, at a high rate of interest. They want universal prosperity; you want general embarrassment. They want to rise to a higher level of civilization; you are hanging on to their legs to pull them down. They desire to work for themselves; you want them to work for you, that you may live in idleness. They are producing, you are consuming; they are creating, you are swallowing; they are the wheat plant, you are the chinch bug; they bless mankind by their work, you benefit nobody but yourself; and in a few short months or years there will be nothing left of you but a coffin full of rottenness; and after all your grabbing you will not be able to pick the worms off your face that are eating away your nose. And if the essence of life is continuous and immortal, you will be then a wretched, unhappy prowler of the spiritual kingdom; or, reincarnated as one of a herd of filthy jack-als, scrambling and fighting for offal."

"What has he when Death forecloses?"

"Thank you," said the peak-nosed man, very red in the face.

"I don't mean to hurt your feelings," said Mr. Sanders, "but have I not told the truth? What have you ever done, or men like you, to merit a moment's kindly consideration from the Lord who made you? With what part of the universal Benevolence, of which this earth is a tremendous testimony, have you ever held a second's communication? What would you do among the blessed saints of heaven, the elect of God, with your present feelings, instincts and impulses? You couldn't get a chattel mortgage on their wings, or foreclose on their golden harps;—and what else would you be capable of thinking about?"

"You have no right to talk that way about me," said the other, "you know nothing of my life or history."

"Well, if I have done you injustice I am sorry for it," replied the farmer. "But Providence is not like the youthful artist who was obliged to inscribe under his sketches: 'this is a pig,' 'this is a house.' The soul writes itself upon its tabernacle, even as the sea-shell adapts itself to the convolutions of the creature that dwells within it.

"But I take it all back. Perhaps every man has to ulfill his destiny, and the wolf and the lamb are made out of the same material; and one could not by any possibility be the other; and even while we defend society, we should therefore be very merciful in our judgment of hose who assail it."

"Dinner ready in the dining car!" cried a young man whose complexion was due to the fact that Noah cursed Ham, for some slight misbehavior, several thousand years ago. But the young man would not have known any-

thing about it if the sons of Shem had not kindly preserved the legend; and the sons of Japhet had not used it
as an excuse for making him work hard for small pay.
But if a man cannot be responsible for the deeds of his
ancestors, 6,000 years ago, what are ancestors good for?

*   *   *   *   *   *

"Mister," said the peak-nosed man after dinner, "do
you know anything about 'trusts?' I should like to hear
something on that subject."

"Yes," said Miss Bowman, "what causes them—how
do they come about?"

TRUSTS.

"They are simply another form of the universal selfishness—'the hog in human nature' I spoke of," replied
Mr. Sanders. "They rest upon the inability of the people
to defend themselves."

"And why is that?" asked a red-headed man, who had
been an attentive listener to the discussion.

"Because," was the reply, "of the inability of the average man to think a new thought that has not got its
roots entangled in a lot of old thoughts. Each age is
therefore the shadow projected by the preceding age—an
incongruous *mixture of errors and truths*. The ancients
believed in the '*mandrake.*'"

"The mandrake? What is that?" asked Miss Bowman.

"You know," said Mr. Sanders, "the great poet says

'Could curses kill as can the mandrake's groan.'

It was the belief that the 'mandrake,' a plant growing in
wet places, and bifurcated like a man, (whence the name
'*man*-drake,') would, when pulled out of the earth, utter
dreadful groans and shrieks, and any one hearing them

would die. And so it was the custom (according to the legends) for the man who wanted the 'mandrake' to loosen the earth around it, tie a stout cord to it, fasten the other end to a dog's tail, get a good distance away and call the dog. Up came the 'mandrake' and the dog died ! Of course all this was false. The 'mandrake' had no more occult power than a turnip; but the human family faithfully believed the yarn for ten thousand years;— which only shows that the human family is capable of believing anything, and that it is safe to doubt anything it believes. Well, what I was going to say, was, that bigotry is the 'mandrake' of the moral world; its roots reach down to the center of the globe; you cannot pluck it up without terrible groanings and shrieks and curses; the very earth comes up with it; and the men who drag it out of its bed generally perish as martyrs for the truth; but when it is once thrown prostrate on the earth it is a poor, mean, shrivelled, nasty, poisonous weed, and the world wonders how it was once capable of so much harm. The 'mandrake' which afflicts this country to-day is party bigotry; the newspapers are the tongue of the thing —full of screams and groans and lies and slanders and imprecations—but the miseries of the unfortunate people are pulling the bigotry out by the roots."

" Party bigotry has rendered the people incapable of self-defense. It blinds them where their eyes should see clearly; it divides them where they should be united; it makes them suspicious of each other when the warmest feelings of brotherly love should prevail among all honest men; it turns their thoughts from their own welfare and the happiness of themselves and families, to old contentions and hatreds, concerning interests and issues long since dead and gone; it makes this lovely world a hell. in

quarrels over the next world, when it is barely possible
there may be no next world; or if there is, that it may
differ as widely from our conceptions as the conditions of
Jupiter differ from those of the earth.   ' Divide and conquer ' is the policy of our plunderers.   ' *Unite and crush* '
should be ours."

Hard Times pulling out the Mandrake of Party Intolerance.

"Have you any statistics," asked Mr. Hutchinson,
"as to the extent of the trusts in this country?"

"Yes," replied Mr. Sanders, "here are some figures
which have been published.   The bankruptcies of some

of the schemers have perhaps modified this table, but it will not, I think, be found far out of the way.

A FEW TRUSTS.

The following are a few of the trusts that have been organized in this country, with their capitalization:

	Capitalization.	Water.
Standard Oil	$ 110,000,000	$ 45,000,000
Cottonseed Oil	41,700,000	25,000,000
American Typefounders	9,000,000	3,000,000
Anthracite Coal	513,000,000	75,000,000
Ax	5,000,000	....
Barbed Wire	12,000,000	4,500,000
Biscuit and Cracker	5,000,000	2,000,000
Brewers (Chicago)	6,000,000	2,000,000
Bolt and Nut	5,000,000	2,000,000
Boot and Shoe	7,000,000	....
Cartridge	3,000,000	....
Condensed Milk	15,000,000	3,000,000
Casket	5,000,000	2,000,000
Celluloid	11,000,000	3,000,000
Cigarette	25,000,000	....
Copper Ingot	20,000,000	....
Cordage	15,000,000	5,000,000
Cotton Duck	10,000,000	2,000,000
Envelope	7,000,000	....
Flint Glass	4,000,000	....
Fork and Hoe	1,000,000	....
Lead	90,000,000	60,000,000
Linseed Oil	18,000,000	12,000,000
Lithographic	11,500,000	....
Locomotive	15,000,000	....
Match	6,000,000	....
Musical Instrument	5,000,000	....
Oatmeal	3,500,000	....
Railroads	10,000,000,000	6,000,000,000
Rice	2,000,000	....
Rubber	60,000,000	23,000,000
Safe	5,000,000	3,000,060

	Capitalization.	Water.
Schoolbook	18,000,000	....
Sewer Pipe	5,000,000	....
Western Union Telegraph	84,000,000	50,000,000
Smelters	40,000,000	....
Soda Water Machinery	9,000,000	....
Spool, Bobbin and Shuttle	7,000,000	....
Starch	10,000,000	3,000,000
Steel	35,000,000	....
Sugar	76,000,000	30,000,000
Trunk	2,000,000	....
Wall Paper	20,000,000	6,000,000
Total	$11,371,700,000	$6,360,500,000

"Look at those stupendous figures," said Mr. Sanders, "eleven billions, three hundred and seventy-one millions, seven hundred thousand dollars of organized capital, and six billions, three hundred and sixty millions, five hundred thousands of bogus capital, or water! It is simply appalling.

"And just think that every dollar of it means an interference with the freedom of trade and market, and the right of a human being to sell where he can sell for most and buy where he can buy for least.

"And this does not include the combines of millers and elevator men, which have been plundering the farmers of the West for the third of a century; or that other gigantic combination of speculators to break down the price of the great staples by option dealings, and false representations, or many others. Even when an anti-trust law was passed by Congress the courts, as usual, riddled it, negatived it and rendered it useless; and when the national government enacted another statute to prevent railroad pooling, the courts again step in, and so twist it around their fingers that it becomes a very means of defense for those

Liberty: *What are you groveling there for? Get up.*

Uncle Sam: *I cannot; my burden is too great.*

Liberty: *How did you get such a load on your back?*

Uncle Sam: *The newspapers kept me shouting, dancing and crowing about the civil war and African slavery, while the rascals heaped these bundles on my back.*

Liberty: *Hold on and I will cut the ropes.*

whom it was intended to restrain; and the only ones who suffer by it are the working people who are trying to exercise a free man's right to keep from sinking into helplessness and degradation. I repeat—this is no longer a Republic, governed by the people, but a Moneyed Oligarchy ruled over by nine judges, selected by the great corporations. And poor 'Uncle Sam,' as we call him, is crawling on his belly, with all that ungodly load of trust-robberies piled on his back.

"And on top of all these burdens they demonetize silver by the aid of British gold and reduce the price of all the commodities by the sale of which our people hope to pay their overwhelming debts."

"I am surprised, said Mr. Hutchinson, "to see so intelligent a man as you are repeating that exploded and demagogic slander about the corruption of Congress by British gold."

WAS CONGRESS BOUGHT TO DEMONETIZE SILVER?

"Well," said Mr. Sanders, "I shall undertake to prove the truth of that charge."

"Now," said the young lady, "the dispute grows interesting. I am ready to believe anything bad of the ruling classes of Great Britain, and I have not much faith in the American Congress."

"In the first place," said Mr. Sanders, "I have shown that the demonetization of silver was a trick."

"How so?" asked the peak-nosed man.

"From the fact that so vast and world-embracing a change was made without a word in the title of the bill or in any part of the bill itself, to indicate or give notice of what was being done. In the second place, it was perpetrated so secretly that the president who signed the bill did not know that it demonetized silver, but many months afterwards congratulated the country upon the large production of that metal, which had been already denied access to the mints by the very bill he had signed! In the third place I have shown that nearly all our leading senators and members, including the speaker of the House, disavowed any knowledge of the real purpose of the bill or of the great change which it had accomplished. They either told the truth and were innocent victims of the wrong, or they were in the conspiracy and paid for shutting their eyes. In the fourth place the act was a trick because it did its work by leaving out of the list of silver coins the standard silver dollar, and doing this in the Senate, after the bill had passed the ordeal of the House, and consummating the great revolution in the darkness and hugger-mugger of a conference report, of six members, in the hurry and confusion of Congressional legislation. In the fifth place, it is shown to have been a trick, and the result of a conspiracy and not an accident, by the fact that from that hour to this, for twenty-two years, the whole power of the American people has been unequal to the task of repealing that law, so surreptitiously born, without a god-father. In the sixth place, if we still have any doubt that this birth of darkness and crime was long gestated, and the fruit of a world-wide combination, we have only to look at the action of the daily press of this country, in almost unanimously defending the nameless and fatherless bastard, by the most ingenious, continuous, adroit and shameless falsehoods; falsehoods for which there is no parallel since God opened his sulphur-hotel for the accommodation of the fallen angels. In fact, in the presence of Prof. Lawrence Laughlin and his kind, Lucifer appears like a very shallow-brained, stupid, commonplace, clownish person-age. He ought to have started a daily paper in heaven in defence of evil, and after one month's publication the Lord would have been so bewildered that he would have said: 'Here Luci, you can take possession. I'll go below!'

"Now," continued Mr. Sanders, "does anybody be-lieve, for one moment, that this concerted cataract and cyclone of misrepresentation could exist *unless it was paid for?* Truth is like the blessed air and the sunshine—it is natural and continuous—because it is in perfect accord with all God's universe;—but falsehood is something ab-normal, unnatural and temporary. Its black waters must be constantly pumped up and forced into the pure current of the world's affairs, and somebody must pay for the pumping; and, if that somebody does not pay, the pump stops and the fetid waters flow back to their native mire in the great swamp, the Serbonian bog, on the borders of Satan's kingdom

" Consider man's struggles with error in the past ages, and think of the terrible array of falsehoods that were poured forth in defence of wrong. Where are they now? You could not reach one of them with an artesian well;—but the face of Truth is as blooming and as beautiful as ever, shrined in the glory of perpetual youth. Think of the arguments for the divine rights of kings, which no less a person than John Milton had to answer; and which are alive yet *even in our own land to-day.* Think of the proofs adduced by the learned, the pious and the wise to prove that the earth did not revolve upon its axis; or the demonstrations made, still earlier, that there was no land where the continents of North and South America now **are.** Think of the innumerable excellent reasons **that**

The Path of Progress—from darkness into light.

were given to prove that the thirteen colonies could not
defeat Great Britain; and of the uncountable lies and slanders against Washington, Jefferson, Adams, Patrick
Henry, and the rest of that noble band of patriots, uttered
by the men who had put a price on their heads. Progress
is simply an exodus out of the tortures of falsehood; and
Truth marches down the ages over the rotten carcasses of
innumerable wrongs.''

''But,'' said Mr. Hutchinson, '' are you not unjust to
the daily press? May they not honestly believe what
they preach?''

'' You defend their character,'' said the farmer, ''at the
expense of their intelligence.   For instance, there has
been a great hubbub over the question of what was the
' unit ' of our currency—gold or silver; and volumes have
been written in the newspapers to demonstrate that it was
originally gold instead of silver.   As Pope says:

> '' ' For thee explain a thing till all men doubt it,
> And argue 'bout it, Goddess, and about it.
> So spins the silk-worm fine her slender store,
> And labors till she clouds herself all o'er.'

''And yet, with all this dodging, trickery, finessing, false
pretenses and false citations, there stood before them, all
the time, the law of 1792, section 9, which reads as follows:

'' 'And be it further enacted, That there shall be from
time to time struck and coined at the said mint, coins of
gold, silver and copper of the following denominations,
values and descriptions, viz.:

'' ' Eagles—each to be of the value of ten dollars *or
units*, and to contain 247½ grains of pure or 270 grains
of standard gold.

'' ' Half eagles—each to be of the value of five dollars,
and to contain 123¾ grains of pure or 270 grains of standard gold.

" ' Quarter Eagles—each to be of the value of $2.50, and to contain 61⅞ grains of pure or 67 4-8 grains of standard gold.

" ' *Dollars or units*—each to be of the value of a Spanish milled dollar, as the same is now current, and to contain 371 4-16 grains of pure or 416 grains of standard silver.

" ' Half dollars—each to be of half the value of the dollar or unit, and to contain 185 10-16 grains of pure or 208 grains of standard silver.

" ' Quarter dollars—each to be of one-fourth the value of the dollar or unit, and to contain 92 13-16 grains of pure or 104 grains of standard silver.'

" Could anything be plainer than this? ' The dollar is the *unit*—' ten dollars or *units;*' ' dollars *or* units;' and then when it comes to declare what the dollar or UNIT is, it enacts that it shall be made of 371 4-16 GRAINS OF SILVER. No gold *dollars* are provided for, and the dollar is the *unit*. And surely there can be no gold dollar units when there are no gold dollars. This is as plain as a pike-staff; and yet the Laughlin breed of prevaricators have covered this whole matter with such a dense cloud of falsehoods that it reminds one of the down east fog, which was so thick that a carpenter shingling a house shingled out onto the fog for twenty feet before he discovered his mistake. The down east fog was thick enough to hold up one carpenter and a row of shingles, but this newspaper fog is intended to be dense enough to hold up the politics of seventy millions of people, and be the formation *for a gigantic fortress of robbery* and oppression."

" But," said Miss Bowman, "you have not yet told us anything about British gold buying up Congress to demonetize silver in 1873."

"Pardon me," said Mr. Sanders, "but this subject is so big that I wander off occasionally."

ERNEST SEYD.

"There was a gentleman who, until recently, resided in Denver, Colorado, named Frederick A. Luckenbach, a man of means; the inventor of a process for crushing ores by pneumatic power; an eminently respectable gentleman. In May, 1892, he went before the Clerk of the Supreme Court of Colorado, and voluntarily made the following affidavit :

"'STATE OF COLORADO, ⎫ ss.
COUNTY OF ARAPAHOE. ⎭

Frederick A. Luckenbach, being first duly sworn on oath, deposes and says : I am sixty-two years of age. I was born in Bucks County, Pennsylvania. I removed to the City of Philadelphia in the year 1846, and continued to reside there until 1866, when I removed to the City of New York. In Philadelphia I was in the furniture business. In New York I branched into machinery and inventions, and am the patentee of Luckenbach's pneumatic pulverizer, which machines are now in use generally in the eastern part of United States and Europe. I now reside in Denver, having removed from New York two years ago. I am well known in New York. I have been a member of the Produce Exchange and am well acquainted with many members of that body. I am well known by Mr. Erastus Wyman.

"'In 1865, I visited London, England, for the purpose of placing there Pennsylvania oil properties, in which I was interested. I took with me letters of introduction to many gentlemen in London—among them one to Mr. Ernest Seyd from Robert M. Foust, ex-treasurer of Philadelphia. I became well acquainted with Mr. Ernest Seyd, and with his brother Richard Seyd, who, I understand, is still living. I visited London thereafter, every year, and with each visit renewed my acquaintance

with Mr. Seyd, and upon each occasion became his guest
at one or more times—joining his family at dinner or
other meals."

"In February 1874, while on one of these visits, and
while his guest for dinner, I, among other things alluded
to rumors afloat, of parliamentary corruption, and expressed astonishment that such corruption should exist.
In reply to this he told me that he could relate facts about
the corruption of the American Congress that would place
it far ahead of the English Parliament in that line. So
far, the conversation was at the dinner table between us.
His brother, Richard, and others were there also, but
this was table talk between Mr. Ernest Seyd and myself.
After dinner ended, he invited me into another room,
where he resumed the conversation about legislative corruption. He said:

"'If you will pledge me your honor as a gentleman
not to divulge what I am now about to tell you while I
live, I will convince you that what I said about the corruption of the American Congress is true.' I gave him
the promise and he then continued: 'I went to America
in the winter of 1872–3, authorized to secure, if I could,
a bill demonetizing silver. It was to the interest of those
I represented—the governors of the Bank of England—
to have it done. I took with me £100,000 sterling, with
instructions that if it was not sufficient to accomplish the
object to draw for another £100,000, or as much more
as was necessary.' He told me German bankers were
also interested in having it accomplished. He said he
was the financial adviser of the bank. He said: 'I saw
the committee of the House and Senate and paid the
money and staid in America until I knew the measure
was safe.' I asked him if he would give me the names of
the members to whom he paid the money—but this he
declined to do. He said: 'Your people will not now comprehend the far-reaching extent of that measure, but they
will in after years. Whatever you may think of corruption in the English parliament, I assure you I would not
have dared to make such an attempt here as I did in your

country.' I expressed my shame to him, for my country-
men in our legislative bodies. The conversation drifted
into other subjects and after that—though I met him
many times—the matter was never again referred to.
                    ' [Signed.]   Frederick A. Luckenbach.
" Subscribed and sworn to before me at Denver, this
ninth day of May, A. D. 1892.
                    " [Signed.]   James A. Miller.
" [Seal.]   Clerk Supreme Court, State of Colorado."

" I am surprised," said Mr. Hutchinson, " that you
quote that letter. It was exploded long ago."

" How ? " asked Mr. Sanders.

" It was shown by a letter of Ernest Seyd's son and
brother Richard," said Mr. Hutchinson, " that Ernest
Seyd was not in America at that time, and hence could
not have bribed Congress; and secondly, that he was
himself a bimetallist, and had written books in favor of
silver, and was therefore not likely to have helped strike
it down."

" I am aware of all that," said Mr. Sanders, " here is
the letter to which you refer.

" ' SIR: Our attention having been directed to statements that have been made in the American press with
regard to the action of the late Ernest Seyd, in 1872, re-
specting the coinage act then pending, you will oblige us
much by giving an unqualified contradiction to these
statements. Ernest Seyd was not in the United States at
that date for the purpose of bribing members of Congress
to vote for the demonetization of silver, never having been
there since 1856. The statement is the more absurd as
he was the first to take up the cause of silver in England
against the prevailing doctrine here, and remained a
consistent supporter of silver, as his numerous works on
the subject will show. We remain,
                    yours truly,   ERNEST SEYD,
                                     RICHARD SEYD.'

" But it will be observed that, while there is a denial of the fact that Ernest Seyd was in the United States in 1872, there is no denial that the Seyd family was well acquainted with Mr. Luckenbach, or that he dined with them in London in 1865; or that Ernest Seyd and he held such a conversation at the dinner table. If Mr. Luckenbach had invented the whole story, if he did not know Ernest Seyd, if he was a fraud, they would have said so most emphatically, for he had assailed the good name of their father and brother before the whole world.

" And if Mr. Luckenbach was an imposter why do we find the following statement recorded in the Congressional Globe, *the official reporter*, as having been uttered in the House, by Mr. Hooper, M. C., Mass., chairman of the Committee on Coinage, which had the bill in charge, April 9, 1872, (Part 3, XLII Congress, 2d session, page 2304):

" ' This bill was prepared two years ago, and has been submitted to careful and deliberate examination. It has the approval of nearly all the mint experts in the country, and the sanction of the Secretary of the Treasury Mr. Ernest Seyd, of London, a distinguished writer, who has given great attention to the subject of mints and coinage, after examining the first draft of the bill, furnished many valuable suggestions which have been incorporated in the bill.'

" But," said Mr. Hutchinson, " the bill was sent to Mr. Seyd in London, and the suggestions made by him were made there."

" Where is the proof of that? " asked Mr. Sanders. " And observe that Hooper says it was ' submitted to nearly all the mint experts in the country.' That is, in the United States. If Mr. Seyd was not in America, why was he the only expert in England to whom the bill was submitted? Why was he PICKED OUT? And is it not strange that the only English expert selected was the same man Luckenbach dined with in London, in February, 1874,---and this fact is not denied by Seyd's relatives,---and to whom Seyd stated that he had been the instrument used by the Bank of England to bribe Congress. The links of connection are all there. Ernest Seyd tells Luckenbach that with $500,000, furnished by the governors of the Bank of England, he had bought the demonetization bill through Congress. 'I saw the committees of the House and Senate,' says Seyd to Luckenbach; and Hooper, chairman of the committee of the House, said on the floor of Congress that Ernest Seyd 'furnished many valuable suggestions' to the committee. Seyd says he 'paid the *money*.' Hooper calls it 'suggestions.' It is a new name for it !"

" But Seyd's relatives deny it," said Mr. Hutchinson.

"If you were to accept the denials of guilt of the convicted criminals, or their friends," said Mr. Sanders, "the prison houses would all be empty."

"But Seyd believed in bi-metalism," replied Mr. Hutchinson.

"And Benedict Arnold," said the farmer, "believed in the American Revolution, but English gold was too much for him, as it was in the other case. It seems to be the misfortune of America that its worst enemy is the country most closely allied to it by the ties of blood, language and institutions. The Revolutionary War is not over yet. The surrender of Yorktown was a mere truce. The aristocracy of England are accomplishing by bribery what it failed to achieve by bullets. We may yet have to meet their corruption with cannon. *They* are honester.'

"But how do you get over the statement of Seyd's

son and brother that he, Ernest Seyd, was not in the United States in 1872 or 1873?" asked the peak-nosed man.

"By the proof that he was here," replied Mr. Sanders, "by the testimony of Hooper first quoted, given publicly on the floor of the House. And furthermore by the testimony of Senator Dawes of Massachusetts, goldite, in the Senate, recorded in the Congressional Record (Part 1, vol. 7, page 125), in which he says Ernest Seyd 'was here at that time, and has been here since,' delivering lectures in the United States. And furthermore, by the testimony of another eminent goldbug, Hon. David A. Wells, who said in the Forum, 'There was a man by the name of Seyd, and he was in this country in 1872.'

"And the late Rev. Gilbert De Lamatyr, Ex M. C., told Mrs. Emery, of Lansing, Michigan, author of that famous little book, 'The Seven Financial Conspiracies,' that Hon. Wm. D. Kelly, M. C., of Pennsylvania ('the father of the House'), told him that he saw the original part of the bill which demonetized silver, and that it was in the handwriting of Ernest Seyd!

"A friend of mine wrote to Gov. Waite of Colorado and asked him what he knew about Mr. Luckenbach. He replied, under date of Denver, Feb. 28, 1894:

"'As to your inquiry about Mr. Luckenbach, he is no myth, but a living entity and resides in Denver. I was introduced to him last year, and he spoke of the fact of his making an affidavit as to Ernest Seyd. He is a very respectable citizen and there is no doubt that every word of his affidavit is strictly true. You are welcome to publish this statement as coming from me, if you choose.'"

"But is Gov. Waite good authority?" asked Mr. Hutchinson.

"The best in the world," replied Mr. Sanders. "You may differ with him in his views; you may regard him, if you please, as extreme, as fanatical; but no man that knows him ever doubted his heroic honesty."

"And you must not forget," he continued, "that Luckenbach's testimony is sworn to; the letter of Seyd's relatives is not. Why, in the name of all that is reasonable, should a wealthy, honorable gentleman, an ex-member of the New York Produce Exchange, not a politician or an office-seeker, go up voluntarily before the clerk of the Supreme Court of Colorado, and make oath to a wholesale lie? What interest had he to induce him to take such a step? What profit would it be to him?

ENGLAND'S INTEREST IN MONOMETALISM.

"But I have shown that the bill could only have passed Congress, in the absence of all public demand, ' with the stealthy tread of a cat,' by the force of corruption; and somebody must have furnished the money, and no small sum at that, to ' sneak ' it through both Houses. Who did it? Who had the interest to do it and the money to do it? Who to-day defends the system thus established and stops the European governments from agreeing to remonetize silver by international action? England. And why does England do this? Mr. Gladstone, with charming frankness, told the whole story when he said that England would never consent to bimetalism because she was the great creditor nation of the globe; that the whole world was in debt to her, and was obliged to pay her thousands of millions of dollars annually, for interest; and, said he, it is England's purpose that the money in which this interest is paid shall be the scarcest and dearest that can be found; because there-

"Opium and Christianity or Die."

with she can buy so much more of the wheat, the cotton, the wool, the corn, the beef, the pork, the tobacco of the nations, at the lowest possible rates.   She can thus supply her own people at half price.   To restore the condi-

"Accept English Monometalism and Die."

tions which existed prior to 1873, would simply be to double England's grocery and butcher's bill; and what is it to England if the whole world sinks into bottomless ruin if only she can survive? The nation that forced opium and missionaries—*in the same treaty*—upon the Chinese, at the point of the bayonet; and whose merchants are now giving away the same deadly drug, by the wholesale, to the Hindoos, in order to cultivate the appetite for the Hell-purveying poison among her own subjecs, would shed no tears if the people of these United States, from ocean to ocean, were starving, or were swimming in a sea of fraternal blood.

THE FALL OF PRICES.

"But," said the peak-nosed man, "you people charge that there has been a constant fall of prices since silver was demonetized in 1873, and my daily paper, 'The Champion Plutocratic Prevaricator,' of Chicago, showed last week that wheat was going up and that corn and pork were higher than they had been for years, while there had been no corresponding change in the price of silver. How do you account for that?"

"Which is the warmer," asked Mr. Sanders, "January or July?"

"July, of course," was the reply.

"You will swear to that?"

"Certainly."

"As long as the observations of civilized man extend, therefore, July has been warmer than January?"

"Certainly."

"And you know you can count upon it," said the farmer, "as a fixed fact in nature, only to be changed by some cosmical catastrophe, that the temperature will increase from late winter to spring and thence to summer?"

"Certainly."

"And yet is there not sometimes a colder day in May than in April?"

"Of course."

"And frosts in June and hot spells in March?"

"Certainly."

"But, nevertheless, the rule, as a rule, prevails, that it grows warmer from February to July."

"Of course."

"Then why is it that we have the colder days?"

"Well, I suppose continuous winds from the north may cause a cold spell."

"Exactly," said the farmer, "or hot winds from the south may make it semi-tropical in January."

"Of course."

"Let me make another comparison," said Mr. Sanders. "Did you ever stand on the sea-beach and watch the tide rising?"

"Yes?"

"Did you notice how sometimes the waves seem to retreat, and you begin to think the tide is falling; but soon in comes another wave that laves the sand a little higher than any of its predecessors; and so—with occasional halts and retrocessions—the great ocean continues to crawl in, until the level is, at last, many feet above low-water mark. Now, what would you think of a newspaper reporter who, observing one of these recessions, should telegraph to his paper:—'Wonderful phenomenon! The tide of the Atlantic stops rising before its time, and the water falls. Has the bottom of the ocean caved in?'"

"I should think," replied the peak-nosed man, "that he was a fool."

"Very right," said Mr. Sanders. "Now suppose you

found that that reporter had furnished his extraordinary statement because he was paid for it, what then?"

"I should say that he was a scoundrel."

"Precisely," replied the farmer. "Now here is a table, compiled from official sources, showing how wheat and cotton and forty-five other principal commodities, fell, side by side with silver, during these twenty-one years. The prices of wheat and cotton are the American market price; the other articles are from the tables of the famous European statistician, Mr. Sauerbeck. Just let me read them to you—they are instructive.

Year.	American computation price of—			European computation— Mr. Sauerbeck's index numbers.	
	Silver.	Wheat.	Cotton.	Index number of 45 principal commodities.	Index number of Silver.
1872	$1.32	$1.47	19.3	....	99.2
1873	1.29	1.31	18.8	....	97.4
1874	1.27	1.43	15.4	102	85.8
1875	1.24	1.12	15.0	96	93.3
1876	1.15	1.24	12.9	95	86.7
1877	1.20	1.17	11.8	94	90.2
1878	1.15	1.34	11.1	87	86.4
1879	1.12	1.07	9.9	83	84.2
1880	1.14	1.25	11.5	88	85.9
1881	1.13	1.11	11.4	85	85.0
1882	1.13	1.19	11.4	84	84.9
1883	1.11	1.13	10.8	82	83.1
1884	1.01	1.07	10.5	76	83.3
1885	1.06	.86	10.6	72	79.9
1886	.99	.87	9.9	69	74.6
1887	.97	.89	9.5	68	73.3
1888	.93	.85	9.8	70	70.4
1889	.93	.90	9.9	72	70.2
1890	1.04	.83	10.1	72	78.4
1891	.90	.85	10.0	72	74.1
1892	.86	.80	8.7	68	65.4
1893	.75	.68	7.2	....	

By this table it appears that silver fell from $1.32 an

ounce in 1872 to 75 cents an ounce in 1893, a fall equal to 43 per cent.; that wheat fell from $1.47 a bushel in 1872 to 68 cents in 1892, a drop of 53 per cent.; and cotton declined from 19.3 cents to 7.2 cents, equal to 60 per cent.

Our Daily Press.

"Observe," continued Mr. Sanders, "that as the swelling tide of the increased purchasing power of gold rolled in steadily for twenty-one years, there were occasional lapses, recessions; but the tide rose, nevertheless. For instance, the increased price of pork is due to the in-

creased price of corn, caused by the greatest failure of the
corn crop last fall, by excessive drought, ever known since
this country was settled; and this drought forced farmers
to sell their cattle; and so cattle are scarce and beef rises;
and the rise in wheat is due to last year's drought and
this year's chinch-bugs, frost and other adverse influences.
" What was it," said Mr. Sanders, turning to the peak-
nosed man, "that you called the reporter who announced
[for money] that the tide was falling before it had half
risen?"

" A scoundrel," said peak-nose.

" Precisely; and can you think of any stronger term to
apply to the men who try to overthrow the force of a
great general truth by the use of petty, temporary subter-
fuges and tricks?"

" The term is strong enough to cover everything,"
said Miss Bowman, laughing.

" Now, remember," continued the farmer, " that these
vile falsehoods and sophistries are perpetrated by men
who call themselves honest, christian gentlemen, and
guides to public opinion in the greatest nation on earth.
They stab their native land and the human family with
one hand, while they hold out the other hand behind
their back to receive the bribe."

SLAVERS.

" But," said the red-faced man, " you must admit that
the Republican party freed four millions of slaves."

" I am not discussing political parties," replied Mr.
Sanders. " There are many noble things in the record of
both the old parties; and the one can point with as much
pride to Andrew Jackson as the other can to Abraham
Lincoln. And yet it is to be doubted whether the new

industrial slavery is not worse than the old domestic
slavery."

" I am shocked to hear you utter such a sentiment,"
said Mr. Hutchinson.

' ' I know you are," was the reply, " but,

> " ' Stone walls do not a prison make,
>   No iron bars a cage.'

"And all of slavery is not the auction block. There are
slaves that wear no gyves; and brains that are lacerated
instead of backs. The black man before the war was
sold to the *highest* bidder; the white slave since the war is
sold to the *lowest* bidder. The master took care of the
first; society takes no care of the latter. The patriarchal
system required the master to nurture the young and
helpless slave, and also those who were too old to support
themselves. The industrial system regards human beings
as the cheapest commodity in the world, because as soon
as one drops off ten stand ready to take his place.
Machinery can not reproduce itself in that fashion; and,
therefore it must be carefully housed and cared for.
Fecund nature supplies men faster than society can
devour them. They are the trash and refuse of the
world."

" But white people are not slaves," said the red-faced
man.

" He is a slave the product of whose toil goes to
enrich another, without any just equivalent to himself,"
replied Mr. Sanders. " No black woman in the South
ever worked as hard in the cotton fields or lived as
poorly as the ' sweaters ' in our great cities. A committee of the New York Legislature was appointed last
winter to investigate the 'sweat shops.' In one instance,
sworn to, and reported in the New York *World* of May

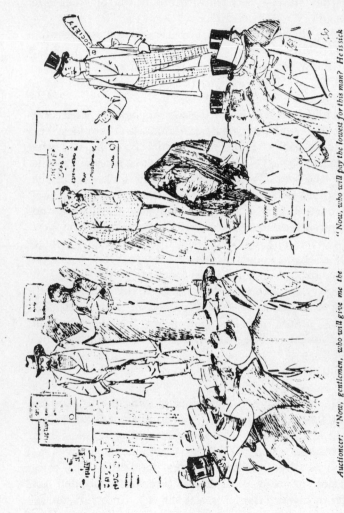

Auctioneer: "Now, gentlemen, who will give me the highest price for this boy? Well-fed, you see, and in good condition. Fine limbed boy. Now bid up lively, gentlemen."

"Now, who will pay the lowest for this man? He is sick and weak and has a family to support. You can get him cheap."

1st, 1895, it appears that a mother and three children, by working hard, *fourteen hours a day*, earned thirty cents a day! Another witness made flannel outing shirts complete for *three cents each*. The work in the week of one man amounted to $4.00; and out of this $2.50 went for rent! Many girls testified they worked for *ten cents a day* !

"Compare these poor, cadaverous, over-worked creatures with the glossy, shining, corpulent black bondsmen of the South, with their gardens, their dances, their songs, their corn-huskings, and their possum-feasts. Why, their lives were a continuous picnic, so far as animal comforts and gratifications were concerned, compared with the inexpressibly wretched creatures in the garrets of New York, working fourteen hours a day for ten cents, and living in clusters like wild beasts; and this not for a day, a week or a month, but for a lifetime. And in the presence of these awful facts religion is silent, while it fingers its salary, and talks about Abraham and Isaac, and ignores the 70,000 prostitutes of New York City alone, whom society condemns to life-long wretchedness here and everlasting tortures elsewhere.

"But you are crying," he said suddenly, turning to Miss Bowman.

"Pardon me," she said, with handkerchief to eyes, "but there came up before me a vision of such a life as you have described—its horrors, its unending horrors —it was like looking into a vista of Pluto's kingdom."

"It is Pluto's kingdom," replied Mr. Sanders. "It is the fruits of Plutocracy; and the question now is in all this fair land, ' Shall Pluto's kingdom cover the continent and be eternal? Or will mankind rise up and drive the demons off the face of the earth ? ' "

"You put it strongly," said Mr. Hutchinson, "but it seems to me you do not approach the real question in all this controversy."

"What is that?"

FREE SILVER WOULD DRIVE OUT GOLD.

"You fail to answer the contention of the single-stand-ard advocates, that the remonetization of silver would give us two kinds of currency, a silver currency worth fifty cents on the dollar, and a gold currency worth one hundred cents; and that this country would become the dumping ground for all the silver in the world, and the gold would be driven out, because gold and silver cannot co-exist side by side."

"Well, well," said Mr. Sanders, laughing, "you have given me a blizzard of conundrums. But I shall try to answer them.

"First, you say, gold and silver cannot exist together. The answer is that they did exist together, among the nations of the earth, for 5,000 years."

"But," replied Mr. Hutchinson, "in our own country gold drove silver out for years prior to the civil war,"

"Why?" said the farmer. "For the reason that silver was at $3\frac{1}{2}$ cents premium on the dollar over gold, because our silver coins were heavier than foreign coins of the same grade; and foreign brokers bought up our silver coins and shipped them abroad to secure the difference. The remedy would have been to reduce the amount of silver in the dollar $3\frac{1}{2}$ per cent., and all temptation to export it would have ceased at once. These are simply small matters, capable of ready adjustment."

"But how about the two kinds of currency if you open the mints to silver?" asked the peak-nosed man.

"Now," said Mr. Sanders, standing up and raising his voice so that every one in the car could hear him, "I desire to put a fair question and I want an honest answer.

THE ARGUMENTUM AD HOMINEM.

"If to-day silver bullion is worth fifty cents on the dollar, and to-morrow the mints are thrown open to silver, and any man can take his silver bullion there and exchange it for legal tender silver dollars, worth one hundred cents, is there any person, within the hearing of my voice, who would sell his bullion for fifty cents on the dollar, or for *anything less than the hundred cents he could get for it at the mints!* Is there?"

There was dead silence. Mr. Hutchinson was engaged studying the scenery.

"I repeat the question again," cried Mr. Sanders, "is there any person big enough fool to take less for his silver than he could get for it at the mint?'

Here a squeaky voice cried out:

"I would."

Mr. Sanders started up the aisle to investigate. He found a sallow-faced young man seated by an elderly lady, who was convulsed with laughter

"*You* would," said Mr. Sanders, looking at the youth, as if about to argue the question with him.

The elderly lady checked her merriment long enough to say:

"Excuse me, sir; don't bother with him. He is my nephew. He is an idiot. I am taking him to the imbecile asylum."

"Ah," said Mr. Sanders, "I thought he was a banker."

"Same thing," said a gruff old fellow, with spectacles, who had listened attentively to the debate; and there was a great laugh, in which Mr. Hutchinson joined heartily.

"Now, gentlemen," said Mr. Sanders, resuming his seat, "you can find nobody but an idiot who would sell his silver bullion for less than free-coinage would give him for it at the mint—to wit: one hundred cents for every 412½ grains of standard silver.

"Well," said the peak-nosed man, "what does that prove?"

"Just this," replied the farmer, "that whenever 412½ grains of silver are worth one hundred cents it is worth as much as the gold dollar. It will perform all the functions of the gold dollar; it has performed them all along; and has been, as a dollar, worth 100 cents, when as bullion it was worth but 50 cents. But the whole cunning cry of the enemies of mankind has been that silver was worth but 50 cents on the dollar, as bullion, because it was shut out of the mints. The moment you throw open the mints to silver the bullion value will raise to the coin value, and there is no power on earth that can keep it down. For no man will sell his bullion at 50 cents when he can coin it and get 100 cents—except our distinguished friend in front, who is on his way to the imbecile asylum. And the proof that silver bullion would rise at once to the value of•the silver coins for which it could be exchanged at the mints, is found in a historical fact. When Harrison was President the U. S. Senate passed a bill to remonetize silver; and it was supposed that the House would also pass it, for there was a large majority in that body in its favor. Silver bullion was then selling for 94 cents an ounce; but inside of ten days it advanced, not in the United States alone, but *all over the world*, to 117—a gain of 23 cents an ounce. If the bill had passed the House it would undoubtedly have risen the other 12 cents necessary to bring it to 128—its old ratio with gold. Silver is depressed in price simply because it is demonetized—the mints are closed against it, there is scarcely any other market for it, except the demand of China, Japan and India. If that was gone it would not be worth as much as pot-metal."

"Why, said Miss Bowman, "did the House not pass the bill?"

"But would not gold, as the superior metal, disappear?" asked Mr. Hutchinson.

"Why should it?" replied Mr. Sanders, "silver would be worth 100 cents and gold would be worth 100 cents; neither, therefore, would be superior or inferior to the other, and there would be no reason why one should drive the other out."

"This is all very well for this country," said Mr. Hutchinson, "but how about foreign nations?"

"Exactly," cried the peak-nosed man, "the English speculator would buy up English silver bullion at 50 cents on the dollar, and bring it over here and take it to the mint and get 100 cents on the dollar for it, and we would be overwhelmed with a flood of all the silver in the world."

"That, I know, is a common argument," said Mr. Sanders, "but let us look into it."

"We will suppose that you, sir," he said, turning to the peak-nosed man, "were in London the day the mints of this country were thrown open to the free-coinage of silver, and you heard silver had risen, at one bound, to 100 cents on the dollar. Now you have a few thousand dollars, and you say to yourself, ' I will buy silver bullion at 50 cents and take it across the Atlantic and coin it at 100 cents.'   And you sally out to find a banker who has silver bullion for sale; and you find him, and a dialogue something like this ensues:

" 'Good morning, sir; I understand you have some silver bullion to sell.'

" 'Yes, I have several million pounds worth of it.''

" 'I want to buy $20,000 worth at 50 cents on the dollar.'

" 'Are you a fool, or do you take me for one? Don't you know that there is such a thing as the Atlantic cable —several of them—and don't you know that the United States have thrown open their mints to the free-coinage of silver, and the holders of the bullion at once put up the price to what they could get for it at the mint; and silver bullion is now worth 100 cents on the dollar.''

" 'But that is in the United States.'

" 'You must be the biggest fool in London. I presume you are an American, belonging to one of the old parties. Don't you know that I can ship my silver bullion over there and get legal tender silver dollars, and buy wheat with them or lend them out on mortgages?'

" 'Then you will not rush your silver bullion over there at once?'

" 'Why should I? Suppose it is worth 100 cents on the dollar on the west side of the Atlantic, then it is worth 100 cents on the dollar on this, the east, side of the Atlantic, less the cost of carriage from England to the United States. Suppose I take a million dollars' worth of silver bullion at the American price and ship it over there and pay the freight, insurance, etc., say one per cent., and get back my 100 cents and my freight, insurance,

etc., what profit have I made by the transaction? My
million dollars are worth a million dollars without carrying them to the American mints.'

" 'Then there will be no flooding of the United States
with European silver?'

" 'Not a flood. That was the kind of stuff we fed the
American fools with, but they got sharp enough to see
through it.'

" 'Well, won't European silver be sent over there?'

" 'There is no European silver, worth speaking of. We
get our supplies from the United States and Mexico. The
latter country always held her silver at 100 cents on the
dollar, and now the United States does the same thing.
We need large amounts of silver annually for subsidiary
coin, and the arts, and we must pay the price demanded
by those who have it for sale.'

" 'Then the price all over the world will be the same?'

" ' Certainly. Is not the price of wheat, corn, meats,
woolens, cotton and everything else the same through all
the markets of the globe, allowing for difference in cost of
transportation from the place of production? Is it possible to conceive of wheat being at the same time, *and con-
tinuously*, worth fifty cents in the United States and a
dollar in Liverpool? Where would the dealers and speculators be? The world to-day is one great shop, knitted
together by telegraph wires, and the price at one end of
the counter is the same as the price at the other end. Go
home to America, young men, soak your head for a week
in fresh milk, don't look at a daily paper for a year, try
to think for yourself, and you may at last rise, by great
effort, above the level of sheer idiocy, into which most of
your so-called business men seem to have fallen. Your
country has long been a field of plunder for the whole

world. It is fast becoming its laughing stock; and your
newspapers and your money-lenders are doing it:—the
latter rob you and the former humbug you;·and you stand
loyally by the chaps who despoil you, and believe en-
thusiastically in the fellows who fool you. You are
a lovely set of daisies to run a great nation. You are the
twentieth trituration of banks, bondholders, foreign capitalists, base-ball games, corrupt newspapers, rotten legislatures, pugilism, corporation judges and bribed jurymen.
Ye are weighed in the balance and found wanting. Your
upper classes despise liberty and the lower classes are per-
meated with discontent, and regard the government as a
sort of slave-driver's whip to make them work without
pay. The great republic is doomed, if there is not salt
enough of virtue among its own people to save it."

Just at this point the cars stopped at a station and·a
telegram was handed one of the passengers. He read it
and sprang to his feet, and waved it in the air, and
shouted : "Hurrah ! The Supreme Court has declared
the income tax unconstitutional."

Every man in the car, except Mr. Sanders and the
gruff gentleman, rose up and cheered, and great excitement prevailed. Mr. Sanders sat in his seat, looking very
much distressed. At last Mr. Hutchinson, whose face
was wreathed in smiles, said to him:

"You don't seem to like it."

"No," replied the farmer, "I do not. It will save
me a little money, but I do not rejoice over that. I am
willing to pay my share of all just taxes, as every honest
man should be. I regret that decision very much."

"Why?" cried the peak nosed man, who was in a high
state of delight.

" Because," said Mr. Sanders, " of its effect upon the country. It will tend still farther to divide the people into classes, and to intensify the discontent of the poorer part of the population, and that way lies death and hell."

" Nonsense," said Mr. Hutchinson.

" I am sorry," said the farmer, " to see in the action of this accidental gathering an evidence of the class feeling already existing, and a proof of the short-sightedness of that class."

" What do you mean by that?" asked the red-faced man.

" You represent the wealthier part of the population," said the farmer, " and you rejoice that you have escaped your share of taxation and thereby increased the burden of those less able to pay than you are."

THE INCOME TAX.

" Well," said Mr. Hutchinson, " we simply utter a natural protest against an unjust system of taxation."

" The income tax," said the farmer, " is the justest mode of taxation known in the world. We already have it in some of the States."

" How so ? " asked the banker.

" In those instances where the State takes a percentage of the gross or net earnings of railroad companies and similar corporations. This is really a tax on their incomes; it is an income tax, and we know of no complaint against it. If you tax personal property it eludes you; it scatters like rats and hides itself. Then you throw the tax upon land, and you thereby punish the farmer for raising food for the world.

" What a man owns is no criterion of what he is worth —it may be covered with mortgages and eaten up with taxes; or it may be for a year, or a term of years, unpro-

ductive. The farmer's crops may be all swept away by
insects, or flattened into the earth by hail, or burned up
by drought; and he may have to borrow money to live;
still the tax goes on. Society adds to the cruelty of
nature, and from the impoverished producer takes his last
dollar. More than that, to collect the tax on land you
have to build up a most expensive, complicated machinery; you employ an officer in each county to make a
list of all the lands in the county, and another set of
officers in each township to assess them, and say what
each piece is worth; then you have to have a county
auditor and a lot of clerks to divide up the tax
and charge against each piece its share; then you
have to have a county treasurer, with another lot of clerks,
to receive the people's taxes; and then you have to
advertise the delinquents so many times in a newspaper,
and hold an auction and sell the property. And *in
many instances the whole tax is paid out for assessing
and collecting it*, and the taxpayers receive little or
nothing for the millions they disburse. And society in
each county is divided into two classes—a tax-paying
class and a tax-eating class. The "tax-eaters" are few
in number, but sharp and shrewd; and as the offices
they hold yield many times more than they could earn in
private life, they are ready to expend a large part of
their salaries to retain them ; and thus the voters are
corrupted and the whole community made rotten and dis-
honest, to the imminent peril of free institutions and the
disgrace of the good name of our country. But, if
there was an income tax levied, we will say, by the state,
and divided among the counties, one set of officers could
attend to the whole business; a whole army of 'tax-
eaters' would be discharged ; and the public would be

purified by the closing up of a thousand fountains of
corruption in each state. Then each citizen would pay
in proportion to what he receives, not in proportion to
what he attempts or hopes to receive. The producers,
the energetic men who create wealth, would be relieved

Poverty: *Kind sir, will you relieve me of a little of my heavy burden?*
Wealth: *Not to-day, sir, not as long as I know any one of the U. S
Supreme Court.*

of their burdens and encouraged; while the idle capitalists, who make hundreds of others work for them, but
do not work themselves, would have to foot the bills.
Taxes are contributions by the people to preserve order
and protect life and property. The poor man does not

need such defence to any great extent. He has nothing for any one to steal. It would profit no man to assail him. But if you refuse to employ policemen and troops in the great cities, or repeal the laws against robbery and murder, a rush of the criminal class would at once be made on the houses of the wealthy, and the lives and fortunes of the Goulds, the Astors, the Vanderbilts and others like them, would disappear in scenes of shocking brutality and carnage. As it is now the few cunning adventurers obtain some advantage, inside or outside the law, and despoil millions to enrich themselves, and then turn around and demand that those they have plundered shall defend them from rapine and outrage, and that they themselves must not be called upon to pay one penny for their body guard. And the Supreme Court of the United States has, by the decision you have been cheering, taken from Congress the power to make them pay anything, and says they shall go Scot-free as long as the nation endures."

"But cannot they be reached by direct taxation?" asked Miss Bowman.

"No; because the constitution says that direct taxes and representation shall both be upon the basis of population; and therefore the poverty-stricken, heavily mortgaged people of the West and South would have to pay as much direct tax as the same number of wealthy people in New England or New York, who own the mortgages; and that would be so shockingly unjust that no one has yet had the effrontery to propose it. This decision you are applauding therefore declares that the great fortunes in this country shall never pay a cent for the support of the government."

"How about the tariff?" asked the red-faced man.

"The very wealthy need pay little or nothing under the tariff. They spend a great part of their time abroad; they are the best customers of English and French tailors and milliners; when they return to the United States they usually come equipped with full supplies of costly clothing that pay no tariff."

"But, can they not be reached by local—state—taxation?" asked Mr. Hutchinson

"They could be if our legislatures were honest," replied Mr. Sanders; "but you know, as well as I, the character of the average American legislator. He spends large sums to be elected, expecting to recoup himself out of the opportunities of his office. He comes prepared to be bribed, and he is not often disappointed."

"You draw a very gloomy picture, sir, of our condition," said Miss Bowman.

"It *is* gloomy," replied the farmer; "it was not so gloomy the week before the battle of Gettysburg. We were not in so much deadly danger then as now. Then both sections were instinct with manhood and heroism; they were volunteers—fighting for principles which they believed to be right; now we have, as a rule, a lot of hireling soldiers ready to shoot down their unarmed fellow citizens, driven by wretchedness to violence and stone-throwing in the larger towns. Then it was an age of splendid heroes; now the community has become so rotten, with universal corruption, that there is scarce coherence enough to hold society together. Instead of heroes we have a lot of emasculated, feminine-like tricksters and usurers. In the last hundred years the resources of this land have been turned into colossal fortunes, which have concentrated in the hands of those who did not produce them; and they are laboring with demoniacal industry and ingenuity to destroy our magnificent free institutions and reduce the common people to European conditions. They do not understand that the American citizen is the old world peasant *plus* generations of training in liberty—he is a new product; nothing just like him has ever been seen before on the face of the earth. He is slow to comprehend the trend of affairs; he can be cajoled through his prejudices and party fanaticism, but when at last it becomes plain, even to his unsuspicious mind, that he is being enslaved, and that his children are to be held in bondage forever, there will come an outburst like the breaking forth of wild beasts. And the longer he is deceived and deluded the more terrible will be the catastrophe when it does come. You men are simply piling up wrath against the day of wrath. And history will record that this decision of the Supreme Court, over which you have been hurrahing, was a most potent factor in making plain to all men that the liberties of the country are already destroyed. Think as you please, write as you please, resolve as you please, vote as you please, formulate your party platforms as you please, fill Congress with your representatives, yet there, high above all the machinery of government, high above your own heads, high above the nation, sit your nine gowned masters, and behind them, shrouded in blood and clouds, is the demoniac spectre of unreasoning human greed— Plutocracy !

" Our fathers dreamed that they could establish on this western continent a nation dedicated to equality, liberty and human happiness. It was for this they labored; it was for this they fought; it was for this they endured untold sufferings. They saw, as in a vision, a mighty brotherhood—none poor, none greatly rich—and over it they lifted up a flag made of stars and lines of light—light for the wretched and unhappy; stars of hope for the downtrodden and the oppressed of all the world.   A little more than one hundred years have passed away, and this is now a land of princes and paupers, of palaces and hovels, of soldiers and tramps, of great wealth and great misery.   All the worst features of European—almost of Asiatic—degeneracy have already appeared among us.   The clamor is already heard for a ' stronger government ' and a larger army; huge fortifications, called armories, have sprung up in all our great cities; and the very children in our schools are being trained, in their callow youth, in the arts and instincts of murder.   While the constitution of the United States declares that no state shall maintain a standing army, large bodies of troops are being organized, uniformed and paid by the several states.   Our legislatures are butcher's shambles, where each piece of meat is hung up and ticketed with its price.   Our politicians clearly understand that subserviency to the power of corruption is the one pathway to wealth and honor; and that he who defends the people must accept poverty and obscurity for his portion; our newspapers, instead of standing on the watchtowers and sending forth ringing bugle blasts to wake and warn the sleeping multitude, are at work, in darkness and night, digging out the foundation walls of civilization, so that the whole grand structure may crumble into ruin at the first shot from the cannon of the enemy.

"On every hand you hear doubts expressed as to the possibility of maintaining republican institutions; with fears of the common peopie—the same common people who formed the nation, and who have ᵈ ᵢfended its life through all the mighty struggles of the past.   A Napoleonic furore has even been surprisingly inaugurated, to dazzle the imaginations of a susceptible race with the tinsel glare of imperial splendors.   The old Tory element which was expatriated to Nova Scotia as traitors, not fit to dwell in a land of freedom, has returned among us and is ruling the country.   The Hamiltonian school of politics, with its aristocratic leanings, its distrust of the people, and its legalized separate costumes for the classes, has taken shelter in the national banks.   The old she-wolf —Nicholas Biddle's bank—which Andrew Jackson wounded, has crawled out of the bushes, followed by all her whelps, and is ravaging the land.

"Oh, my friends, it is useless to argue longer about petty details, as to "units" or statutes, or dates, or figures. Clearer than the difference between blackest night and brightest day is the difference between the two policies now presented to the American people.   The one leads us back into the horrors of the past—irresponsible masters— kingship--the rulers brutes—the people serfs—the bayonet of greed at the throat of the thinker—humanity prostrate, degraded, helpless.   The other policy points forward toward the dawn of the world's perfect morning —universal prosperity; universal happiness; no violence; no proscription; no intolerance; no darkened minds; no broken hearts; labor no longer starving, and idleness gorging; but peace, plenty, equal opportunity and fair play over all the earth.

"That is night and its horrors.   This is day and its glories.

"Choose ye between them.

"The bell tolls the hour of destiny and doom.,

DATE DUE